THE ART
OF
X-RAY READING

THE ART OF X-RAY READING

HOW THE SECRETS OF 25 GREAT WORKS OF LITERATURE WILL IMPROVE YOUR WRITING

ROY PETER CLARK

LITTLE, BROWN AND COMPANY
New York Boston London

Little, Brown and Company
Hachette Book Group
1290 Avenue of the Americas, New York, NY 10104
littlebrown.com

First Edition: January 2016

Little, Brown and Company is a division of Hachette Book Group, Inc.
The Little, Brown name and logo are trademarks of Hachette Book Group, Inc.

The publisher is not responsible for websites (or their content)
that are not owned by the publisher.

The Hachette Speakers Bureau provides a wide range of authors for speaking events.
To find out more, go to hachettespeakersbureau.com or call (866) 376-6591.

ISBN 978-0-316-28217-8
LCCN 2015942281

10 9 8 7 6 5 4 3 2 1

RRD-C

Printed in the United States of America

To my brothers, Vincent Clark and Ted Clark,
for their tender care of our mom,
Shirley Clark, who, at age ninety-five, was still singing.

CONTENTS

X

Contents

THE ART
OF
X-RAY READING

Where Writers Learn Their Best Moves

Where do writers learn their best moves? They learn them from a technique I call X-ray reading. They read for information or vicarious experience or pleasure, as we all do. But in their reading, they see something more. It's as if they had a third eye or a pair of X-ray glasses like the ones advertised years ago in comic books.

This special vision allows them to see beneath the surface of the text. There they observe the machinery of making meaning, invisible to the rest of us. Through a form of reverse engineering, a good phrase used by scholar Steven Pinker, they see the moving parts, the strategies that create the effects we experience from the page—effects such as clarity, suspense, humor, epiphany, and pain. These working parts are then stored in the writer's toolshed in boxes with names such as grammar, syntax, punctuation, spelling, semantics, etymology, poetics, and that big box—rhetoric.

Let's get to work.

Please put on your new X-ray reading glasses so we can examine the titles of a couple of famous literary works. The first is "The Love Song of J. Alfred Prufrock" (1915), by T. S. Eliot. (The poet died in 1965, my senior year in high school, when I became the keyboard player in a rock band called T. S. and the Eliots.)

"Prufrock" is widely considered one of the great poems of the twentieth century, and I encourage you to read it for the first time, or again, to see if my claims about the title ring true. The poem is, most of all, a poignant reflection on the losses brought on by aging. The protagonist is torn between the lingering longings of youth—romance, sexual energy, creativity, social prominence—and his sense of himself as an old man. He wonders if women at social gatherings, discussing Michelangelo, will notice him; he shrinks in stature and wears his pants rolled up at the cuffs; he worries whether his dentures will allow him to eat a peach. He looks back to see how his life has been "measured out," a wonderful poetic phrase, and all he can see is coffee spoons.

Those are the dramatic and thematic outlines of the poem, but how did Eliot create them? If we can answer that question, perhaps we can begin to know some of the things he knew as a writer. Maybe there will come a time when we can reach for that knowledge and write a title to a text that draws on the same creative energy used by Eliot.

So what is the source of that energy?

My X-ray vision reveals that "The Love Song of J. Alfred

Prufrock" is a title built upon a tension, a friction, a rub between two dramatically different phrases, two radically different kinds of language.

Write down some of the associations you make when you hear the phrase "love song." My list contains courtship, romance, flirtation, beauty, serenade, youthful exuberance, hope, longing, music, poetry. The range of associations — writers call them connotations — can be wide. A Shakespeare sonnet is a love song: "My love shall in my verse ever live young." But so is "Double Shot (Of My Baby's Love)," by the Swingin' Medallions.

So who is the persona created by Eliot to sing his love song? Does he have a poetic name such as Marvell, Wordsworth, or Longfellow? No: his name is J. Alfred Prufrock. Make a list of things that come to mind when you read or hear that name. My list includes banker, academic, attorney, businessman, bureaucrat. Nothing defies romance like a name that begins with a first initial followed by a full middle name. John A. Prufrock sounds more regular than J. Alfred Prufrock, which tiptoes near a parody of cold British fussiness. And then there is Prufrock, a name in full defiance of "love song." Passion and fervor are neutralized by the empiricism of *Pruf* (proof) anchored to the hardness of *rock*. Read another way, that last name might divide as Pru-frock — someone who wears prudish or prune-ish garb, a shrinking old man who wears his trousers rolled up so he won't step on them.

The tension can be felt in the very letters. The first phrase — "love song" — hooks up the liquid consonant *l* with the sexy sibilance of *s*. In contrast, Prufrock links a plosive *p* with the fricative *k* sound. Combined, the effect is like a great wave of sea and sand crashing onto a boulder-blocked shore.

See what happens when you put on those X-ray glasses? You are cured of the myopia of common reading. Beyond clarity, you gain an inner vision of literary effects, at its best psychedelic, kaleidoscopic, and 3-D. You are beginning to see as a writer.

Let's say you've learned that lesson—that a gifted writer may create a title in which two key elements collide. You now see titles in a new way. Another Nobel laureate, Thomas Mann, penned a novella entitled *Tonio Kröger*, published in 1903. This was one of the first stories I read in college under the tutelage of a brilliant young scholar named Rene Fortin. (He also assigned "Prufrock" as part of our required reading.) He taught us how to pay special attention to moments of tension in a text.

Such tension was easy to find in the character of Tonio Kröger, a young man torn between the influences of his German father and Italian mother. He imagines his life as an artist, a life of sensual creativity, the part he inherited from his mother. But he has elements of his father in him, too—a German banker whose life, however dull, offers the promise of stability and financial security.

"I want you to feel that tension in Tonio Kröger," lectured Fortin. "Feel that collision between the coldness of his northern European heritage and the heat from the Mediterranean south. It's there before your eyes, there before you read the first word of the story." We had no idea what he was talking about, but he was right: there it was in the title itself—*Tonio Kröger*. Italian versus German. Long, open vowels versus umlaut and hard consonants. An artist's first name versus a banker's last name. To my ears, Tonio has the sound of a romantic character in an Elizabethan play. Kröger sounds like a form of currency.

X-ray reading not only gives you deeper reading knowledge, it also gives you a writer's knowledge. Think now of all the authors who have created titles, popular and literary, in which two elements don't feel as if they belong together. My favorites include:

Paradise Lost
The Adventures of Huckleberry Finn
The Catcher in the Rye
To Kill a Mockingbird
"Leda and the Swan"
Dr. Jekyll and Mr. Hyde
The Postman Always Rings Twice
Who's Afraid of Virginia Woolf?
The Great Gatsby

But to those classic works of literature I would add popular ones such as the Harry Potter series. J. K. Rowling's powerful young wizard has an English king's nickname and a common tradesman's last name. How about popular reality shows such as *Duck Dynasty* and *Amish Mafia*? My favorite title, as you may know by now, is *Buffy the Vampire Slayer,* in which the savior of mankind, the one who defeats the forces of evil, is not a Conan or a Van Helsing but a blond teenage Valley Girl named Buffy. It is as odd a title as if Melville had made his famous whale purple and named it *Moby Grape* (actually the name of a 1960s San Francisco–based country-rock band).

Hey, I want to play.

I heard that one of the top executives at Little, Brown—my publisher—had been reluctant to publish my book on the elements of language, a sequel to *Writing Tools*, until he was dazzled by my title, *The Glamour of Grammar*. There you go again. What could be less glamorous than the common perception of grammar? And yet at one time in the history of English, they were the same word, as odd a combination as if T. S. Eliot had named his love song "Tickle Me, Elmo."

The idea for this book was born during the summer of 2013 on the Long Island Railroad. Because the new film version of *The Great Gatsby* had just come out, I was reading the novel for the sixth time. Six readings, as you will see in the next chapter, really tunes up your X-ray vision. By the time I arrived at Little, Brown's offices on Park Avenue, I was on fire with new insights into this classic American novel. My personal copy was marked up with circles, arrows, and endless notes in the margins.

"It's as if you were undressing Gatsby," said my editor, Tracy Behar.

"Undressing Gatsby," I repeated.

"That could be the title of your next book," she said.

"Undressing" was Tracy's sweet synonym for "X-ray reading." My slight preference for X-raying comes from a desire to see the skin of the story—yes, freckles, pores, hair follicles, and all. But I also want to be able to see the bones, ligaments, tendons, muscles, organs, and all the inner workings of the body.

We will begin by undressing *Gatsby,* then *Lolita,* then twenty-three more classic and influential works of literature. Many of you will be familiar with these works, even if you read them back in your high school or college days. I hope you will be inspired to read them again. If you have not read them, or even if you have never heard of them, not to worry. I will provide enough in the way of summary, background, and direct quotations for you to catch up and keep up. Following each X-ray reading will be what I call moments of discovery transformed into lessons. These are writing strategies that can be extracted from the text for immediate placement in your toolshed. Once you experience these moments, your reading and your writing will never be the same.

1

X

X-raying *Gatsby*
Power of the Parts

Like so many others, I was introduced to *The Great Gatsby* in high school—just about the time the Beatles arrived in America. Because I went to high school on Long Island, I was curious about F. Scott Fitzgerald's transformation of Great Neck and Sands Point into West Egg and East Egg. Beyond that, the book was lost on me. I lacked the experiences of impossible love and incalculable wealth. I had not yet acquired the critical capacity to appreciate the book's lyrical sentences. When a teacher ranked it near the top of modern American novels, my response was, "You mean that's the best we can do?"

As I was writing this chapter, I heard National Public Radio book critic Maureen Corrigan testify to a similar lack of enthusiasm for *Gatsby* in her first high school reading, an opinion since transformed by her more than fifty readings of the book. Her experience led her to write a perceptive tribute to *Gatsby,* entitled *So We Read On.* I have at least forty-four readings to go until I catch up with her!

With age and multiple readings comes insight. What do I see in the novel that I was blind to fifty years earlier? The author remains the same (still dead); the text—in spite of disagreements among editors about the author's intentions—has been established (very much alive); so I, the reader, become the X factor. Or should I call it the X-ray factor? One change in me is significant. I now think of myself as a writer. What follows, then, is a practical reading of the text—not a grad student's or lit teacher's or postmodern scholar's—but a writer's reading of *The Great Gatsby.* What can I learn from the novel that I can apply to my next story? How can the book become for me—and for you—a mentor text?

I could choose countless passages to study, as many bright and shiny things to admire as decorated Gatsby's mansion. I could have great fun picking at the author's naming of people, places, and things; connecting the images related to eyes—from the faded billboard ad for the eye doctor to the owl-eyed man at Gatsby's funeral; discussing the archetypal tensions between the promised land and the wasteland, as experienced in the "valley of ashes"; studying Fitzgerald's intentional elaborations on classic themes of American literature, patterns of individual and collective greed and renewal that can be traced back to Franklin, Emerson, Hawthorne, and Whitman.

Instead of those, I'll start with the end, one of the most revered passages in literature, so revered that the 2013 movie version spelled it out on the screen. To fully appreciate it, you might borrow a trick from my old friend Steve Lovelady and copy it out by hand. "I want to get the feel of what it's like to have that prose flowing through my fingers," he would say. This passage is four paragraphs long, the 273 words coming from narrator Nick Carraway, who stretches out on the shore of Long Island Sound and gazes out at the water:

Most of the big shore places were closed now and there were hardly any lights except the shadowy, moving glow of a ferryboat across the Sound. And as the moon rose higher the inessential houses began to melt away until gradually I became aware of the old island here that flowered once for Dutch sailors' eyes—a fresh, green breast of the new world. Its vanished trees, the trees that had made way for Gatsby's house, had once pandered in whispers to the last and greatest of all human dreams; for a transitory enchanted moment man must have held his breath in the presence of this continent, compelled into an aesthetic contemplation he neither understood nor desired, face to face for the last time in history with something commensurate to his capacity for wonder.

And as I sat there brooding on the old, unknown world, I thought of Gatsby's wonder when he first picked out the green light at the end of Daisy's dock. He had come a long way to this blue lawn, and his dream must have seemed so close that he could hardly fail to grasp it. He did not know that it was already behind him, somewhere back in that vast obscurity beyond the city, where the dark fields of the republic rolled on under the night.

Gatsby believed in the green light, the orgastic future that year by year recedes before us. It eluded us then, but that's no matter—to-morrow we will run faster, stretch out our arms farther...And one fine morning——

So we beat on, boats against the current, borne back ceaselessly into the past.

Before I answer the big structural question—where did that ending come from, and how does it fit in with the whole?—I want to spend some time with its fine details, an X-ray reading meant to discover some of the strategic treasures inside, treasures that could brighten the work space of any writer.

COMMON OBJECTS WITH DEEP MEANINGS

One of my first great literature teachers was a Catholic priest named Bernard Horst, who taught us two key lessons that have stuck with me since high school. "Boys," he said during a reading of a Robert Frost poem, "sometimes a wall is more than a wall. Sometimes it's a symbol." But when we started seeing symbols everywhere, he cautioned: "Careful, boys: a symbol need not be a cymbal."

So is that ferryboat out on Long Island Sound a symbol? If so, it does not crash or sizzle in our consciousness like a drummer's cymbal in a jazz band. That ferryboat is much more subtle stuff—a half symbol, perhaps, or maybe just a normal object that in the context of the story is fraught with connotation.

Rides on ferries remain part of the life of many who live on Long Island and in the New York City metropolitan area.

The Staten Island Ferry may be the most famous, but ferry-boats still carry passengers across the Long Island Sound from towns such as Port Jefferson and Orient Point to places in Connecticut.

The problem that confronts the curious reader, of course, is that the ferryboat is also an ancient literary type. In Greek and Roman mythology—and in Dante's *Inferno*—the dead (and sometimes the living) travel via ferry down into the underworld, also known as Hades, or hell. The ferryman has a name, Charon, and, if you pay him, he will carry you in his boat across the river Styx, which divides the world of the living from the world of the dead. In ancient Greece, coins were placed in the mouth or on the eyes of a dead person to provide "cab fare" for the journey into the next world.

In other legends a dead hero—King Arthur, for instance—is placed on a boat, loaded with riches for the next world, then buried or cast off to sea.

Let's remember what precedes this passage: the murder of Gatsby and a depressing funeral, attended by a handful of people. The appearance of the ferryboat at the beginning of this passage strikes a somber note. It denotes, then connotes, a journey through darkness, the end of life as we know it, followed by transport into an uncertain future.

SYMBOLIC GEOGRAPHY

Islands are celebrated in life and in literature, perhaps because great cultural centers—Japan, England, and Manhattan—are islands. Think of all the jokes and riddles and stories you know about being lost or abandoned on a desert island, from

Robinson Crusoe to *Gilligan's Island*. Think *Treasure Island*. Think *Lord of the Flies*. And remember that, according to John Donne, no man—or woman—is an island.

Islands are natural microcosms, little worlds inhabited by a limited number of players, whose actions, values, and behaviors come to represent universal conflicts. Long Island is a very distinctive island shaped like a fish, more than one hundred miles long and twenty miles wide. It takes up most of the distance between the Empire State Building and the Montauk lighthouse. It is so big, in fact, that it does not serve as much of a small symbolic universe for Fitzgerald. His preference is to go smaller, not with one but two miniaturized worlds in conflict: East Egg and West Egg, where old-money and new-money interests clash.

Like many great writers, Fitzgerald is tuned in to what I might call symbolic geography, not just in the settings of the two Eggs but also in the journey (by auto or train) from Long Island to Manhattan through an industrial wasteland referred to as the valley of ashes. The road between mansions and skyscrapers turns out to be a journey through the underworld, a descent into hell. Only bad things happen to characters who end up there or pass through it.

The simple mention of the Dutch sailors, European explorers who settled New Amsterdam, evokes the mixed heritage of Western history, in which the "new found land" is imagined as a paradise found, a place of endless territory, wealth, and possibility. It will flower for the new settlers trying to escape their pasts in the Old World, but the virgin land will be deflowered by violence and greed.

RECURRING IMAGE

Authors have lots of ways to help the reader understand what *they* think is really important. They do it by word choice, for example, or word order. They do it by repetition. Smokey Robinson wrote "My Girl" for the Temptations and created such an effective lyrical hook that the phrase is repeated more than thirty times in a song that lasts less than three minutes. Yes, damn it, he's talkin' about "my girl, my girl, my girl…"

I learned this lesson—call it the echo effect—in my first college literature class. We were reading one of those thick Russian novels, and our professor asked us to analyze a passage in which a character was disturbed by a fly. I remember going through the novel looking for some clue to unlock this passage, and the best I could do was make reference to an earlier passage in which another fly had made a cameo appearance. "To understand what was happening in this passage," I offered in class, "I thought I might compare it to the passage where the fly made an earlier landing." That was it. That's what the teacher was hoping we would discover.

At first glance, "green breast of the new world" appears to be Fitzgerald's synonym for the original unspoiled America, colonized by the European explorers and settlers. But there is something suggestive and troubling about that "green breast." There is an immediate tension, a rub, between the two words. A green breast is a surreal, almost unnatural thing—unless we are talking about Dalí paintings or cartoon ogres. Then we must ask, where do those words come from in the novel? What are their antecedents? The color green is easy, with its evocation of the green light at the end of Daisy's dock. That light is what T. S. Eliot would call the objective correlative, the object that correlates to all of Gatsby's regrets, dreams, and aspirations. *Breast* is more troubling. Is the word associated with the female objects of desire in the book—Daisy Buchanan and Jordan Baker? Early on, Nick describes the athletic Miss Baker as "small-breasted." But much later—and more shockingly and memorably— comes an image of violence and catastrophe, the effects of the hit-and-run killing of Myrtle Wilson: "…when they had torn open her shirtwaist, still damp with perspiration, they saw that her left breast was swinging loose like a flap, and there was no need to listen for the heart beneath." That phrase occurs on page 137 of my edition, late enough to be well remembered by a reader who encounters that "green breast" only forty-three pages later.

EXAMPLE TO MEANING

In 1939 a language teacher in Chicago published a book for his college students that remains a classic. The author was S. I. Hayakawa, an expert on semantics (the meanings of words), and the book was *Language in Action*. In that book, Hayakawa introduced to American readers a concept called "the ladder of abstraction." The basic notion was that you could think of a word or phrase—his was "Bessie the cow"—and you could place it near the bottom of the ladder, where words referred to concrete, specific things: "Sadie's wedding ring" or "the broken headlight on Karen's dark green 1966 Mustang convertible" or "that 1956 Mickey

Mantle baseball card—the one with the bent corner—that Roy kept in an old shoe box in his attic for more than fifty years." These are objects that appeal to the senses. Gatsby's yellow car, Daisy's green light, Myrtle's bloody breast—all these would be placed at the bottom of Hayakawa's ladder.

What happens in life and literature, of course, is that these objects come to mean something more. Over time, they may take on new meanings. Perhaps the author chooses them to help the reader reach a higher understanding. Even without such authorial intention, the text can come to mean something at a higher level of abstraction. A hundred readers may come away with a hundred different ideas.

This passage in *Gatsby* begins with a sweeping recollection of the "vanished trees" that once seduced the European settlers with their majesty, beauty, and fecundity. This land will be ravaged by those settlers; the trees will disappear to make way for Gatsby's extravagant mansion; the natural world will be despoiled by the artificial.

The narrative suddenly gains altitude, the language soaring to the level of ideas, with phrases such as "transitory enchanted moment," "aesthetic contemplation," and "capacity for wonder." Such phrases stand atop the ladder of abstraction, inviting the reader to strive for some higher understanding of the characters in this particular story and their connection to the larger, deeper themes of American history and culture.

It astonishes me how Fitzgerald manages to compress the complex and contradictory concerns of American history and culture in a single passage. His main vehicle for this is a constant movement—from concrete to abstract, from particular to general. After offering us a contemplation of what the sailors must have felt when they encountered the islands and forests of the New World, the narrator connects that sense of "wonder" (and repeats the word) by recalling what Gatsby must have felt when he looked out at Daisy's dock and saw the green light.

Gatsby is seduced by a dream: that he can go back in time, erase the past, and begin again in the arms of Daisy. It is interesting to note the collision of colors here, the proximity of the green light to the blue lawn. Shouldn't the lawn be green? Isn't grass green? Not in Gatsby's world. In his world of unnatural aspiration, the grass must be greener than green. It must be blue, as blue as the blood of aristocrats.

RIGHT WORD

In rereading my 2004 edition of the book, published by Scribner, I thought I found a misprint: "Gatsby believed in the green light, the orgastic future..." *Orgastic?* Is that even a word? I checked an earlier edition and found the word as I remembered it. Not *orgastic* but *orgiastic*. I looked up *orgastic* and found that it was an obscure synonym for *orgasmic*. It carried a meaning beyond sexual pleasure—a higher and deeper level of ecstasy. Did Gatsby believe in an ecstatic future?

According to Fitzgerald scholar Matthew J. Bruccoli, the author indeed meant *orgastic* and discussed it with his editor, Maxwell Perkins. But in 1941, editor Edmund Wilson thought the word was an error and replaced it with *orgiastic,* which became the version known to a half century of readers. Fortunately, *orgastic* has been restored and was the word spoken by Nick Carraway in the movie. Why fortunately?

Not just because it was the word the author intended but also because it is just the right word. Given the Jazz Age orgies of sex, booze, and excess described in the novel and magnified in the movie, it is easy to be seduced into thinking that Gatsby believed in an orgiastic future. But we know that he threw those parties for one reason and one reason only: to find Daisy — or to create the circumstances in which she could find him. It was a much more personal ecstasy he believed in and was striving for.

RULES TO TOOLS

One of the delights of studying the work of a great author is to stumble upon glorious experiments in punctuation. Most of us learned punctuation prescriptively, as a set of rules that help point the reader to a particular meaning. Where do I pause? Enter the comma. Where is the thought completed? Enter the period, or what the Brits call the full stop.

Once a writer learns the conventions of punctuation, he or she is free to bend them for creative purposes. I often ask students in writing workshops to punctuate Henny Young-man's famous one-liner "Take my wife, please." Do a Google search and you will find these alternatives:

Take my wife. Please.
Take my wife — please.
Take my wife, PLEASE!

The urgency of pleading will determine the choice of punctuation.

From humor to art:

> It eluded us then, but that's no matter—to-morrow we
> will run faster, stretch out our arms farther...And one
> fine morning——

I remain in awe of this passage, of its stretched-out ellipses and its extended dash, which seems to point to nowhere—or to infinity. The dream unfulfilled. The poison of regret. Ecstasy interrupted.

STORY ARCHITECTURE

So far, this close reading has focused on the textual elements, but it's time to shift to structural, or architectural, concerns—the ways in which the patterns of language and imagery create the backbone of a narrative. I would say it's almost impossible to perceive these patterns in a single reading: it took me six to understand their full effects.

Where did that ending, that contemplation of the green light, come from? Books have endings, but so do chapters. The seeds for the ending of *Gatsby* are planted at the end of chapter 1, where Nick sees Gatsby for the first time:

> But I didn't call to him, for he gave a sudden intimation
> that he was content to be alone—he stretched out his
> arms toward the dark water in a curious way, and, far as I
> was from him, I could have sworn he was trembling.
> Involuntarily I glanced seaward—and distinguished noth-
> ing except a single green light, minute and far way, that

might have been the end of a dock. When I looked once more for Gatsby he had vanished, and I was alone again in the unquiet darkness.

It's all there: the dark water, the green light, the end of a dock, the stretching, reaching, and desperate striving—as well as the elusive character of Gatsby. The title of the novel, *The Great Gatsby,* strikes many as a kind of oxymoron: that is, Gatsby seems a clumsy surname for someone great, like *The Great Lipschitz;* but the title also has the feel of a magician's name, like the Great Houdini. The word *vanished* seems just right.

Should a reader at the end of a 180-page novel be expected to remember that foreshadowing passage on page 21? Maybe. But perhaps the reader could benefit from a reminder. I found it in the novel's central scene, in which Gatsby and Daisy are reunited after five years, thanks to the maneuverings of Nick Carraway.

"If it wasn't for the mist we could see your home across the bay," said Gatsby. "You always have a green light that burns all night at the end of your dock."

Daisy put her arm through his abruptly, but he seemed absorbed in what he had just said. Possibly it had occurred to him that the colossal significance of that light had now vanished forever. Compared to the great distance that had separated him from Daisy it had seemed very near to her, almost touching her. It had seemed as close as a star to the moon. Now it was again a green light on a dock. His count of enchanted objects had diminished by one.

It is important to note the repetition of key words over significant spaces of text. The word *vanished* echoes the end of chapter 1, Gatsby's vanishing act. But *enchanted* anticipates the phrase at the end of the book, "a transitory enchanted moment."

It just so happened that I was visiting Long Island while I was rereading this passage—I couldn't have been more than ten miles from the imaginary West Egg—when I noticed that it fell on page 92. That is, page 92 of a 180-page novel! The physical, structural, virtual center of the novel.

What are we to learn from this? It should remind us that a truly great work of art is exquisitely and finely wrought. It should reveal how purposeful is the strategic vision of the author. Whatever its effect in *Gatsby,* it also serves as a writing lesson for the rest of us, whether we are writing fiction, nonfiction, memoir, screenplays, or poetry.

WRITING LESSONS

1. Common objects—the sea, the ferryboat, the forest, the moon, a steeple—can resonate subtly in stories and lend texture to your meaning even though they may derive from classic symbols or archetypes.

2. Stories have settings, of course (such as the north shore of Long Island in the Jazz Age). But the internal geography of a narrative can convey its own associations and influences, from the insularity of an island to the wasteland of an industrial heap to the golden metropolis to an artificial paradise. Let the landscape—in all its variety—tell its version of the story.

3. If you have a key word or phrase in a work of any significant length, remember that its repetition will magnify its significance and help readers connect various parts of a story.

4. When you want readers to see with their senses, use specific concrete details, images, and examples. When you want them to reflect, climb up the ladder for language that conveys ideas.

5. When you have a fabulous and memorable word or phrase—such as "capacity for wonder"—place it strategically at the end of a sentence or, better yet, a paragraph. Followed by white space, this language stands out from the rest, inviting the reader to pause and complete the thought.

6. Your writing should move, move, move. From concrete to abstract. From specific to general. From idea to example. From information to anecdote. From exposition to dialogue. A good book is a perpetual motion machine that drives a story and lets the reader feel the energy.

7. Words have denotations—their literal meanings—but also connotations, which are their associative meanings. There is no better way to illustrate this than through colors. Green is green, a visual perception. Daisy's light is green. But think of all the associations that come with that color: the natural order; full speed ahead; money, money, money; but also inexperience, nausea, envy, and greed. The lawn is blue—a color we usually associate in a positive sense with sky. Here it conjures up warped values and a closed society.

8. Mark Twain was right: the difference between just the right word and almost the right word is the difference between lightning and the lightning bug. Be adventurous

with words—even invent new ones. But beware of misunderstanding or overinterpretation, either by readers or editors.

9. Take command of the conventions of typography and punctuation, but realize they can function as rhetorical tools and not just rules. Some ancient examples of punctuation come from scripts for actors in which the writer or director helps the actor figure out the points of emphasis and the dramatic pauses. Used purposefully, punctuation can help you build elements of suspense, surprise, delight, confusion, delay, and much more.

10. The big writing lesson is this: if you have some very powerful idea or image—something of great interest and importance—introduce it early in the work, bring it back into view in the middle, and reveal its great power at the end.

2

X

X-raying *Lolita*

Words at Play

I was a college student when I read *Lolita* by Vladimir Nabokov for the first time. I borrowed the book from the library. I remember this because early in the book a previous reader— a woman, I presume—had made a lip print on one of the first few pages, as if she were blotting her lipstick. The color was a vivid red, and its sudden appearance added another level of outlawed sensuality to the experience of reading.

Sue Lyon was fourteen years old when she was cast to play Lolita on the big screen. Her obsessed older lover, Humbert Humbert, was played by the oh-so-elegant James Mason. Stanley Kubrick's movie, released in 1962, made it difficult to remember that the narrator-protagonist was a pedophile, the object of his desire being not a physically mature adolescent but a girl who was barely twelve years old. Sue

Lyon, with her heart-shaped sunglasses and her cherry lolli-pop, seemed older. The lip print in my library book could have been hers. So for me, *Lolita* was fully sanctioned and eroticized.

I am looking at the novel now through a different lens—X-ray vision, a writer's eye. I am trying to experience it in a way that Nabokov himself describes in *Lectures on Russian Literature:*

> Literature, real literature, must not be gulped down like some potion which may be good for the heart or good for the brain—the brain, that stomach of the soul. Litera-ture must be taken and broken to bits, pulled apart, squashed—then its lovely reek will be smelt in the hol-low of the palm, it will be munched and rolled upon the tongue with relish; then, and only then, its rare flavor will be appreciated at its true worth and the broken and crushed parts will again come together in your mind and disclose the beauty of a unity to which you have contrib-uted something of your own blood.

Give me a moment to express my amazement that a tri-lingual author, born in Russia and fluent in French, could write such a lush and lyrical passage in English. It has been said—appropriately, I think—that the novel *Lolita,* also written in English, is a kind of love letter to the language. Some find its style too ornate, too rich. To me it feels more like it was written by a child who grew up with eight crayons and had just been given a box of sixty-four. All those colors — the burnt sienna and the aquamarine — creating dazzling effects that are evident on every page. *Lolita* is a language playground.

In no text is that clearer than in its famous opening passage:

> Lolita, light of my life, fire of my loins. My sin, my soul. Lo-lee-ta: the tip of the tongue taking a trip of three steps down the palate to tap, at three, on the teeth. Lo. Lee. Ta.
>
> She was Lo, plain Lo, in the morning, standing four feet ten in one sock. She was Lola in slacks. She was Dolly at school. She was Dolores on the dotted line. But in my arms she was always Lolita.
>
> Did she have a precursor? She did, indeed she did. In point of fact, there might have been no Lolita at all had I not loved, one summer, a certain initial girl-child. In a princedom by the sea. Oh when? About as many years before Lolita was born as my age was that summer. You can always count on a murderer for a fancy prose style.
>
> Ladies and gentlemen of the jury, exhibit number one is what the seraphs, the misinformed, simple, noble-winged seraphs, envied. Look at this tangle of thorns.

If you are counting, those 169 words fall into four paragraphs, each one with a special emphasis, moving down a corridor of language past these big rooms: Sound, Names, Story, Meaning. Let's examine each one for its rhetorical and strategic purposes and effects.

SOUND

I am no linguist, but I've always been alert to letters and sounds and how they are formed in the English speaker's mouth. Some consonants — such as *s* and *z* and *sh* — seem to sizzle in the mouth, like Parseltongue, the snake language of the Harry Potter stories. These form a group called the sibilants. So when Nabokov writes "My sin, my soul," he creates a sound with friction, two different words, *sin* and *soul,* rubbing against but trying to escape from each other.

E. B. White tried to play out the effects of repeated sibilants with this showy passage: "The South is the land of the sustained sibilant. Everywhere, for the appreciative visitor, the letter 's' insinuates itself in the scene: in the sound of the sea and sand, in the singing shell, in the heat of sun and sky, in the sultriness of the gentle hours, in the siesta, in the stir of birds and insects."

Let's consider the sounds formed by the letters *d* and *t* in the phrase that Kramer, in a famous episode of *Seinfeld,* uses to describe Jerry (because of his disdain for dentists): "anti-Dentite." No surprise: the sounds made by the tongue against the back of the teeth are called interdental. Those occur in the *Lolita* passages, too — not just in the final syllable of her pet name or in the first letter of versions of her given name, Dolores, but also in the alliterative string "the tip of the tongue taking a trip of three steps down the palate to tap, at three, on the teeth." If you are counting, that's eight taps of the *t* sound, if you include the last syllable in *palate.*

So far we've covered the sibilants and the interdental sounds, but let's not forget the most erotic letters and sounds of all—the liquid consonants *l* and *r*. To roll out these sounds requires good use of the tongue, and Nabokov requires us to taste the name of his obsession: "Lolita, light of my life, fire of my loins." So much happens in those nine words, which technically qualify as an intentional fragment, or verbless sentence. Notice how the three-syllable name generates eight one-syllable words. Notice how the words *light, life,* and *fire* all repeat that long vowel sound. Notice the parallel framing of those two appositive phrases: "light of my life," "fire of my loins." It must be said that *loins* manages somehow to be a crude euphemism (how's that for an oxymoron?). It refers to the male genitals, but in a way that evokes a side of beef.

As I was writing this, I came across a *60 Minutes* interview between Anderson Cooper and the white rapper Eminem. In spite of a miserable childhood that had him moving from school to school in urban Detroit—repeating the ninth grade three times—Eminem said that he always liked the study of English. He opened a file box that was filled with clippings of experimental rhyme, hundreds of pages of what he referred to as his ammo. No rhyme is impossible, he declared, if you shape the words in your mouth and deliver them with the right beat, which is why the supposedly unrhymable *orange* met its match with both *door hinge* and *syringe* in the songs "Business" and "Brainless." Such creativity by Marshall Mathers (Eminem—get it?) is ludic in nature, work discovered and expressed in play.

NAMES

The power of *Lolita* is so great that the character's name now appears in dictionaries. The eleventh edition of *Merriam-Webster's Collegiate Dictionary*, referencing the novel, defines "Lolita" as "a precociously seductive girl." *The American Heritage Dictionary* prefers "a seductive adolescent girl." It should not surprise us that New York tabloids referred to the teenage Amy Fisher, who shot the wife of her lover in the head, as the Long Island Lolita. Those liquid consonants are hard to resist.

A scientific classification is called a taxonomy, and there is something of that in Nabokov's breakdown of the various names of the girl who was born Dolores Haze. Her last name is brilliant enough, given Humbert's state of mind. The litany of her names reveals one powerful expression of his fixation. The girl is so various and splendid a creature that she cannot be confined to one name. Nabokov was a famous lepidopterist, and there is something of the butterfly collector in these names, each one describing a different stage in her development: Lo, Lola, Dolly, Dolores (on the dotted line!), Lolita. Notice the continuing tension between the liquid sounds and the hard sounds. One gets the sense of a butterfly floating out of a cocoon.

By the second half of the novel, Humbert is on the lam with Lolita, cruising across the country, taking refuge in a never-ending cavalcade of motels, roadside attractions, and cheap eateries. Humbert brings his Old World sensibilities to his interpretation of homogenized America: "…all those Sunset Motels, U-Beam Cottages, Hillcrest Courts, Pine

View Courts, Mountain View Courts, Skyline Courts, Park Plaza Courts, Green Acres, Mac's Courts."

Place names and tourist attractions stand out like stars: Blue Licks, Poplar Cove, Little Iceberg Lake, Bear Creek, Soda Springs, Painted Canyon, Shakespeare, Conception Park.

It starts with Genesis, of course—the idea that human beings have dominion over nature because of their ability to name things. The poets have special power. Many high school students skim over book 2, lines 603–611, of the *Iliad,* which to the uninitiated may seem like a miasma of names of ships, tribes, and warriors. Up close, those names signify centuries of history, mythology, and culture:

> They who held Arkadia under the sheer peak, Kyllene,
> beside the tomb of Aipytos, where men fight at close quarters,
> they who dwelt in Orchomenos of the flocks, and Pheneos,
> about Rhipe and Stratia and windy Enispe;
> they who held Tegea and Mantineia the lovely,
> they who held Stymphalos, and dwelt about Parrhasia,
> their lead was Angkaios' son, powerful Agapenor.
> Sixty was the number of their ships, and in each ship
> went many men of Arkadia, well skilled in battle.

Given the revered status of all these classic texts, I am disinclined to hold my own writing up for inspection, except to note one occasion on which I was clearly influenced by the classification of names at the beginning of *Lolita*. I was writing about famed Penn State football coach Joe Paterno. The context was his fall from grace as a result of a child-sexual-abuse scandal involving his former assistant, which rocked the campus and the football program:

> If I didn't know Joe Paterno was a real person, I would swear he was invented, a character in a sports adventure novel written for boys in the 1950s. There he'd stand on the sidelines, hands behind his back, squinting in the sunlight, Joe Paterno, legendary coach at State College, the beacon of moral and physical courage, the shepherd of lost boys, pater familias in a place called Happy Valley.
>
> An author could not invent a better name: Joe Paterno. St. Joe, father of a holy family of student athletes. JoePa. Papa Joe. Pater, as in Latin for father. Eternal paternal Paterno.
>
> Our father, who art in trouble, hollow be thy name.

Naming, of course, emerges as a thematic problem in *The Great Gatsby*. Jay's family name, we learn, is Gatz — too short and too ethnic, perhaps, to fulfill the protagonist's romanticized sense of himself. Changing his name to Gatsby becomes an act of reinvention very much in the American grain — and, to cite a much older transformation, very much like the way Saul becomes Paul in the New Testament.

In a revealing passage, Nick Carraway keeps track of those attending Gatsby's lavish parties by inscribing their names and circumstances on the empty spaces of an old wrinkled railroad timetable:

> From East Egg, then, came the Chester Beckers and the Leeches, and a man named Bunsen, whom I knew at Yale,

and Doctor Webster Civet, who was drowned last summer up in Maine. And the Hornbeams and the Willie Voltaires, and a whole clan named Blackbuck, who always gathered in a corner and flipped up their noses like goats at whosoever came near. And the Ismays and the Chrysties (or rather Hubert Auerbach and Mr. Chrystie's wife), and Edgar Beaver, whose hair, they say, turned cotton-white one winter afternoon for no good reason at all.

This catalog proceeds for about three pages and offers a kind of flyover view of the social order in Gatsby's corner of Long Island, akin to Homer's naming of the ships and Chaucer's naming of the pilgrims. Fitzgerald's method seems to be to create a string of interesting names, adding a juicy detail or two, saving the most interesting detail until the end of a paragraph: "and Henry L. Palmetto, who killed himself by jumping in front of a subway train in Times Square."

STORY

So far, we've examined this famous passage from *Lolita* for the power of its sound imagery and its use of names. But euphony and taxonomy do not a story make. There is a hint of story—of characterization—in the details of Lolita's dress: the one sock and the slacks as well as her place in Humbert's arms. But these are just teases.

A true narrative—the kind we expect in a novel—has some true requirements: a narrator, for example; scenes with dialogue; rising and falling action; an arc; an inciting incident; a climax; a denouement. In a writing guide, these are jargon words. They can only be put into action by authors telling stories, and authors have to begin somewhere.

The third paragraph of the *Lolita* excerpt acts as a compass, carrying the reader from the alpha point in the story (the tragic death of a young girl whom Humbert loved in his youth) to the omega point (his murder of the defiler, Clare Quilty). It may seem like some violation of narrative theory to essentially give away the murder element of the plot in the third paragraph of the novel. But there are many precedents for doing so. I have on occasion drawn distinctions between "What" narratives and "How" narratives, and it may be worth doing so here. The "What" narrative drives the reader or movie viewer to find out what happens next. This is the essential characteristic of a page-turner such as *The Da Vinci Code,* which may not contain a single memorable sentence but whose plot twists and mini cliffhangers drive the reader to the next chapter.

But what happens when you read *The Da Vinci Code* for the second time? Or *Gatsby* for the sixth? Or when you watch *Star Wars* for the fiftieth time? We already know what happens in the narrative, but there is still great pleasure in reimmersing ourselves in *how* it happens.

Consider the first eight lines of *Romeo and Juliet:*

Two households, both alike in dignity,
In fair Verona, where we lay our scene,
From ancient grudge break to new mutiny,
Where civil blood makes civil hands unclean.
From forth the fatal loins of these two foes
A pair of star-crossed lovers take their life;

Whose misadventured piteous overthrows
Doth with their death bury their parents' strife.

It is quite remarkable to see Shakespeare laying out not just the arc but also some of the key details of the narrative that is about to be performed. Chances are, too, that the story of the "star-crossed lovers" was known to the audience from earlier poems and love ballads, both in English and Italian.

Why would Shakespeare bother to write the play if he tells us what is to happen in the first eight lines—almost like a news story? The answer says everything about the power of story, about a writer's ability to render experience in a way that seems real, so that the death of the lovers, when it comes, hits us as a shocking surprise, even if we know it's coming, even if we've seen—to quote a line that comes later in the play's prologue—the "two hours' traffic of our stage" a dozen times.

We learn from Humbert that there is a backstory to his narrative of Lolita. There was another "girl-child," somewhere long ago, in "a princedom by the sea." That language speaks of fairy tales, of summer love, but also of wolves lurking in dark woods, of innocence betrayed.

MEANING

It's been a while since we've seen that fourth and final paragraph that begins *Lolita,* so here it is again:

> Ladies and gentlemen of the jury, exhibit number one is what the seraphs, the misinformed, simple, noble-winged seraphs, envied. Look at this tangle of thorns.

The brief journey from sound to names to story moves us to the meaning, or the engine, of the novel. By using the word *engine*, I refer to Tom French's definition of what drives the reader through the story: it is a question that can only be answered by the story itself. "Who will finally sit on the Iron Throne and rule Westeros?" Or, more simply, "Who committed the murder?" Or "Who will win the race and get the girl?" It's more complicated in *Lolita*, but it is telling that Humbert would shift from the sensual language of love to the formal language of law. We already know that he has a sexual obsession with a young girl and that he has committed a murder because of it. He frames his predicament as though he were a narrator on trial before a jury of his readers.

As evidence, he will present his first exhibit, which I assume is Lolita as seen through his eyes. There is a bit of "surprised by sin" going on in this passage (to borrow a phrase from Stanley Fish). The idea is that even seraphs—the highest order of angels, who sit in the very presence of God—are seduced by the object of desire who is Dolores Haze on the dotted line. If the angels cannot resist her, then how can the imperfect Humbert? We are back to sounds again, an essential tension between the sibilant seraphs and the tangle of thorns that constitutes the tortured life.

WRITING LESSONS

1. Language exists first as a set of symbolic sounds. Written language comes much later to signify those sounds, twice removed from the thing itself, a sign of a sign. Stay in tune with the oral and aural forms of stories. When you find

strong passages such as the ones in this book, read them aloud before you X-ray them. Then stay in the habit of reading your own texts aloud (a) to hear strengths and weaknesses, (b) to test for rhythm and tone, (c) to hear the voice, and (d) to play the music of the words.

2. In your research, hunt for and gather the names of the things you write about. Get the name of the dog, the make and model of the sports car, the brand of the beer. Ask over and over: What is that called? Does it have a name? Names have a special language and cultural power when expressed in lists, catalogs, phone books, litanies, yearbooks, rosters, ships' logs, and blogs. A name is a tool to project an overview of character, ethnicity, generation, gender. When you are reading fiction, imagine that every syllable of every name has a meaning. Why does the lover of Lolita have the same first and last name?

3. In your reading and writing, zero in on the kind of narrative before you. A What narrative requires elements such as cliffhangers to propel the reader from one part to another; a How narrative, in effect, gives away the ending, or at least seems to. When that ending becomes known early to readers, it propels other questions. Not just how but also why.

4. Meaning is secured at the end of a reader's journey through a text. Ask yourself if your work has an engine, a question that can only be answered by continuing to read the story to its end. We want to know who will live and who will die; who will win and who will lose; who will wind up in the mansion and who is headed for the poorhouse.

3

X

X-raying Hemingway and Didion
Words Left Out

Writers of my generation—the baby boomers—grew up being told that Ernest Hemingway was a great writer. We read his books, such as *The Old Man and the Sea,* as early as junior high, and our first inklings of authorial style came from the legendary writer's pellucid prose. There was also a macho bravado surrounding Hemingway, a personal narrative of great adventures around the world that lent his work an additional muscularity.

A typical tribute came from the author Ford Madox Ford, who, in a 1932 introduction to an edition of Hemingway's first successful novel, *A Farewell to Arms,* wrote:

Hemingway's words strike you, each one, as if they were pebbles fetched fresh from a brook. They live and shine, each in its place. So one of his pages has the effect of a brook-bottom into which you look down through the flowing water. The words form a tessellation, each in order beside the other.

It is a very great quality.

The word *tessellation* means "mosaic," and it is the kind of word (like my *pellucid*) that Hemingway might not have used when a more common one was available.

In the harsh light of such glowing tributes, it became our job to kneel at the altar of Papa Hemingway and to worship passages such as this famous one, which opens *A Farewell to Arms,* a novel set in Italy during World War I:

> In the late summer of that year we lived in a house in a village that looked across the river and the plain to the mountains. In the bed of the river there were pebbles and boulders, dry and white in the sun, and the water was clear and swiftly moving and blue in the channels. Troops went by the house and down the road and the dust they raised powdered the leaves of the trees. The trunks of the trees too were dusty and the leaves fell early that year and we saw the troops marching along the road and the dust rising and leaves, stirred by the breeze, falling and the soldiers marching and afterward the road bare and white except for the leaves.

I can say now that as a young reader and writer I did not get Hemingway at all. My negativity may have been nothing more than a 1960s rebellion against the sensibilities of our parents. I could see why Shakespeare was great—and Chaucer, too. But Hemingway was the same age as our parents, and if they liked him it was evidence that something was wrong. I liked Little Richard, not Patti Page.

While some would claim that the passage above is strong, clear, lean, direct, and pure, all I could see was dry, repetitious, undecorated, and dull, a movie star without makeup. My problem, of course, was that I did not yet own a pair of X-ray glasses. I wasn't reading closely enough.

WHAT'S THERE AND WHAT'S MISSING

To my rescue came another great American writer, Joan Didion, an important literary stylist in her own right who has mastered forms as diverse as novel, memoir, essay, and screenplay. When an unfinished novel of Hemingway's came out in 1998, Didion wrote about it in *The New Yorker* magazine. It was a dazzling essay that began with the excerpt from Hemingway quoted above. What follows is her remarkable X-ray reading of the text, not from the perspective of a critic or scholar but that of a fellow writer. She is clearly looking deep beneath the surface of the text, and she does it in a single long paragraph:

> That paragraph, which was published in 1929, bears examination: four deceptively simple sentences, one hundred and twenty-six words, the arrangement of which remains as mysterious and thrilling to me now as it did when I first read them, at twelve or thirteen, and

imagined that if I studied them closely enough and practiced hard enough I might one day arrange one hundred and twenty-six such words myself. Only one of the words has three syllables. Twenty-two have two. The other hundred and three have one. Twenty-four of the words are "the," fifteen are "and." There are four commas. The liturgical cadence of the paragraph derives in part from the placement of the commas (their presence in the second and fourth sentences, their absence in the first and third), but also from the repetition of "the" and of "and," creating a rhythm so pronounced that the omission of "the" before the word "leaves" in the fourth sentence ("and we saw the troops marching along the road and the dust rising and leaves, stirred by the breeze, falling") casts exactly what it was meant to cast, a chill, a premonition, a foreshadowing of the story to come, the awareness that the author has already shifted his attention from late summer to a darker season. The power of the paragraph, offering as it does the illusion but not the fact of specificity, derives precisely from this kind of deliberate omission, from the tension of withheld information. In the late summer of *what* year? *what* river, *what* mountains, *what* troops?

That analysis turns out to be one of the best X-ray readings I have ever encountered, so granular that I am now fixated on the *and*s and *the*s, so persuasive that I am reading Hemingway with fresh eyes. Cheers, Papa: because of Ms. Didion you've made it into this book.

EMPTY SPACES, FULL OF MEANING

When something is overdesigned, we often criticize it as being too busy or cluttered. The same is true of the arts. First it was Miles Davis and then Tony Bennett who preached the virtues of knowing which musical notes to leave out. Didion is so tuned in to Hemingway that she can see the small deletions, which can create a big effect.

It is not obvious why the deletion of *the* before *leaves* makes such a big difference, but it does. Perhaps the effect upon the reader comes from the establishment of a pattern followed by a variation of the norm. Notice that the word *leaves* appears four times in the passage, in three cases preceded by the definite article *the*. In the third example, *the* disappears, only to be restored in the last two words. The author sends out lots of signals that *leaves* is important, including repeating it four times, then letting it stick out at the end of the paragraph, abutted to the white space.

So what is the difference between "the leaves" and "leaves"? Perhaps it is the difference between specificity and generality. Between things that are contained within a space or moment and those that suddenly appear. *The* defines certain leaves that are covered with dust and fallen. Without it, I get a greater sense of chaos—once-living things scattered to decay.

Sometimes in stories, leaves are not just leaves. Falling leaves are a convenient and ancient emblem for the loss of life and the change of seasons. They may be dropping from the trees between summer and winter. But remember that the dust of the roads coats the leaves, acting, perhaps, as a kind of environmental defoliant. And where does that dust come from? From troop movements. Why are the troops there? To wage war. And what does war do? It tramples everything, kills everything. So maybe the dust is not just dust at all. Maybe it's an iconic symbol of mortality. Dust to dust.

For those unfamiliar with the plot, this is the story of an ambulance driver during World War I who is injured, meets a nurse, falls in love with her, and impregnates her only to see her and the child die in childbirth. It is so dark an ending that the character played by Bradley Cooper in *Silver Linings Playbook* flips the novel out the window in disgust after reading it. Sorry, Bradley: you, too, are dust.

REPETITION, NOT REDUNDANCY

Redundancy is built into the English language, helping us derive meaning from even imperfect prose. One of my favorite songs goes, "I gotta girl named Bony Moronie. She's as skinny as a stick of macaroni." It's so much fun to see the same concept—ultra thinness—reinforced by four different words: *bony, skinny, stick,* and *macaroni.* While redundancy works especially well in songs and spoken language, in written texts it can get annoying. If someone writes, "The spy peered furtively through the bushes," our inclination is to hunt down that unnecessary adverb and kill it. For goodness' sake, if he's a spy and he's peering through bushes, isn't his furtiveness understood?

Almost the opposite of redundancy is purposeful repetition. Truly distinctive words, such as Hemingway's *powdered* above, deserve their own spaces. But there is no need to strain yourself looking for synonyms for *river, house, road, leaves,* and *dust.* These words form the foundation for the passage, and their repetition falls on the reader like a drumbeat. *River* and *house* are repeated twice. More important words—*road* and *dust*—occur three times. And perhaps the most important noun, *leaves,* rings four times. One solid variation is when *troops,* mentioned twice, become *soldiers* by the end, as if an indistinguishable group becomes individualized as it approaches and passes.

Another form of variation allows key words to come together toward some parallel structure, as in these phrases in the final sentence: "troops marching," "dust rising," "leaves...falling," "soldiers marching."

The simplicity of the words finds a counterpoint in the length of the sentences. They run from twenty-six words to thirty to twenty to fifty. The length of that final sentence mimics the marching of the troops, which is an excellent match of form and function. The short sentence may sound like the gospel truth. The long sentence takes us on a journey.

Two qualities stand out about the diction, or word choice, in this passage. One of them, as Didion points out, is brevity. Most of the words consist of a single syllable, something that's easier to find in English than, say, in Italian, because our language draws from Anglo-Saxon, or Old English, with its many single-beat words. After 1066, that language would be invaded by Norman-French, adding a rich inventory of polysyllables and Latinate abstractions to the mix, so that by the time Chaucer was writing in 1380, he had a treasure chest at his fingertips. Hemingway seems to prefer Anglo-

Saxon in his choice of words such as *house, dry, dust, white, trees, road, breeze,* and *leaves.* (I checked, and all these are derived from Old English except *breeze,* which may derive from the Spanish *bris.* Short words can find their way into English by various paths.)

In addition to their brevity, the words in this passage are marked by their plainness and commonness. In spite of the sophistication of Hemingway's novel in terms of theme and characterization, there is no word in the passage that would not be recognized by an average elementary school student. Perhaps the most "literary" word is the descriptive metaphor *powdered,* which is a substitute for, say, *dusted.* If I had to choose the most important word, the obvious answer would be *leaves* because of its emphasis, repetition, and thematic foreshadowing. A subtler answer would be *afterward.* As an adverb — often characterized as a weak part of speech — this may seem a surprising candidate. Except for this: it is the only three-syllable word in the passage and as such stands out from the rest. In the land of the monosyllable, the trisyllable modifier gains a kind of stature. More important is its meaning. *Afterward* signifies the state of the world subsequent to the movement of troops, leaving only the symbols of death in their powdery wake.

This landscape at the front door of the novel bears a bitter fruit at its end, when the protagonist will lose a stillborn child and then its mother. Very big things, like the death of humans in a big war, can be prefigured by little things, like dusty leaves upon the ground. Love, sexual union, and the creation of new life could have been an antidote to the pervasive poison of war, but not in Hemingway's view of the world.

As I was writing this chapter, *The American Scholar* magazine ran a brief feature called "Ten Best Sentences," selected by their editors. I noticed that one of the sentences was written by Joan Didion; it appears in her book *Slouching Towards Bethlehem:*

> It was the United States of America in the cold late spring of 1967, and the market was steady and the G.N.P. high and a great many articulate people seemed to have a sense of high social purpose and it might have been a spring of brave hopes and national promise, but it was not, and more and more people had the uneasy apprehension that it was not.

Perhaps I was drunk on Hemingway at the time, but I see in Didion's sixty-seven-word sentence a familiar pattern. The passage is more abstract than Hemingway's. There are no roads, rivers, houses, trees, or leaves covered with dust. There is not much to see. But most of the words are short and simple. *The* is repeated four times, as is *and,* which acts like the coupling link between railcars. Just as there is a tension in Hemingway between the natural order and the machinery of war, there is in Didion a kind of nihilism in the repetition of "it was not" and in the negation of "brave hopes" and "high social purpose." I can well imagine Didion reading the passage from Hemingway and then writing her own.

WRITING LESSONS

1. As important as what to put in is what to leave out. This is easy to say but hard to do. After you've written a draft, read it aloud, but only to yourself. If you read it to someone else, that person may ask questions, which will lead to a longer draft. That can make things clearer. But if your goal is spare prose, it helps to listen for the useless or distracting word or phrase. It may *look* right on the page. But when you *hear* it, it may sound like that extra note in a trumpet solo.

2. Repetition is different from redundancy. Don't strain yourself looking for synonyms. I'll point this lesson out several times in this book. Think of repetition as a drumbeat. Somehow, a marching drummer can repeat a rhythm countless times without making it sound tedious. After a while, the rhythm becomes unnoticeable, almost like a heartbeat. But it must be done for effect and with a purpose. Beware of those times when you unintentionally repeat a word or image. Readers will judge you as inattentive.

3. The big words count, but so do the little ones. I'll demonstrate this by revising my last sentence: Big words count, but so do little ones. I like that better, I think. It feels plainer, somehow, and more direct. Yet the definite article *the* expands the effect of the words it modifies, perhaps by emphasizing the parallel distinction between "the big words" and "the little ones."

4. Hemingway's dusty landscape should remind us that a setting can be symbolic. In the summer of 2014, I began to notice how many news stories involved violence,

or attempted violence, in elevators. I realized that an elevator—even with its compression of time and space—is an effective setting for certain kinds of stories. It is a box of fears: of heights, of enclosed spaces, of crowds. It reminded me how often authors choose certain kinds of spaces—the garden, the dungeon, the tower chamber, the cave—to pressurize human action. These enclosed spaces are often balanced against much broader symbolic landscapes, such as oceans, mountains, deserts, or swamps. As I think of the television series *Breaking Bad,* I remember the tension created when the protagonists, Walter and Jesse, built a meth lab in the confines of a trailer, then drove it out for privacy and security into the barrenness of the desert.

4

X

X-raying James Joyce
Language as Sacrament

I hold in my hand the first book I ever studied in a college English class. It's *Dubliners* by the Irish novelist James Joyce, a collection of loosely connected stories set in and around the Irish capital early in the twentieth century. The next novel we read in class was *A Portrait of the Artist as a Young Man*, the magical and rebellious story of Stephen Dedalus and his Irish Catholic boyhood. I am not Irish myself, but I was very Catholic, educated by Irish nuns and brothers, so I delighted in the story of young Stephen, who would one day escape Ireland—as did Joyce. "I go," writes Stephen at the novel's end, "to encounter for the millionth time the reality of experience and to forge in the smithy of my soul the uncreated conscience of my race." (I just discovered, by accident, that this famous line is exactly 140 characters long. *A Portrait of the Artist as a Young Tweeter.*)

Wow, I thought when I read that for the first time. What an ambitious vision for a young man. And how different from my goal at that age—which was to get a date.

It just so happened that on my honeymoon, in Montreal—on August 13, 1971, to be precise (I have the receipt)—I purchased a copy of Joyce's novel *Ulysses,* which a Canadian customs officer considered a candidate for confiscation. (Because of its stream-of-consciousness sexual content, especially Molly Bloom's "Yes" soliloquy, *Ulysses* appeared on many lists of banned books.) As a young scholar devoted to Joyce, I became attached to his dazzling experiments with fiction and thematic critiques of Catholicism and, most of all, to his mesmerizing adventures with language. If Shakespeare brought poetry to the stage, Joyce brought poetry to English prose, challenging the reader to experience the text on at least two levels—on the level of story and again on the level of text—even challenging us to go beneath the text to discover the invisible ink that lights up the page. Getting to that deeper level requires...what else? X-ray reading, of course.

NAMES AND MYTHS

Let's begin with the name Stephen Dedalus. It seems perfectly made, constructed from two conflicting storytelling traditions: Catholic hagiography and Greek mythology. In the Christian scriptures, Stephen is considered the first martyr, stoned to death for his fidelity to Jesus. He is also associated with Christmas, his feast day celebrated on December 26. Remember "Good King Wenceslas looked out / On the feast of Stephen"?

Dedalus in Homer and the myths of ancient Greece is a maker, an engineer, a builder, a blacksmith. In one story he constructs the great labyrinth that contains the Minotaur. In another he crafts a set of wings for his son, Icarus, connecting the feathers with wax. In spite of his father's warning, Icarus flies too close to the sun, the wax melts, and he plunges into the sea to his death, one of the great parables about ambition.

The key to the ancient Dedalus is that he is a smith, a maker, as is the character Stephen, as was Joyce himself. A maker of poems and stories. A maker of meaning. With an ambition as dangerous as that of Icarus: "to forge in the smithy of my soul the uncreated conscience of my race." That danger is hidden in the astonishing infinitive "to forge," which can mean "to form by heating and hammering"—as a blacksmith does—or "to imitate falsely"; "to counterfeit." It's not quite a contranym, one of those strange words in English that carry opposite meanings, such as *cleave* and *sanction*. But the two meanings of *forge*—like molecules—bump into each other, causing friction and heat.

WORD HOARDS

A detailed study of an author's language, like the one in the last section, comes under the rhetorical rubric known as diction. By *diction* here we do not mean the clarity with which words are pronounced. We mean the feel and effect of the writer's vocabulary as a whole. The diction in *The Adventures of Huckleberry Finn* is consistent with that of an uneducated eleven-year-old boy living in a certain part of Missouri before the Civil War. The diction of *The Catcher in the Rye*, whose narrator is a troubled high school kid living in New York City early in the 1950s, has the ring of authenticity to it. Control of diction helps the writer with focus, theme, tone, setting, time, and much more.

Let us, for a moment, compare and contrast the diction of three important writers of the twentieth century: James Joyce, Philip Roth, and Salman Rushdie. They share, among other things, a deep connection to a religious culture. Far from being orthodox, they spend or spent their work lives challenging the traditions in which they were raised. To quote a priest friend of mine, they are members of a tribe who spend their lives asking nasty questions about God. In college, I wrote a paper describing Roth's *Goodbye, Columbus* as an "anti-Jewish Jewish novel." I could say something similar about Joyce's narrative on Irish Catholicism and Rushdie's view of Islam in *The Satanic Verses*, for which he received officially sanctioned threats of assassination.

But it would surprise me if Joyce built his work on allusions connected with Islam or if Roth's work depended on the sacramental language of Christianity. There is instead an identifiable collection of words—the Anglo-Saxon poets called it a word hoard (like a treasure chest)—drawn authentically from the experience of growing up in a certain cultural tradition. It must be said that such a language heritage is only influential and not determinative. It can be enhanced and enriched by education and travel. But it cannot be escaped. It should be embraced.

Let's turn our X-ray eyes on the famous passage that begins the novel *Ulysses*.

Stately, plump Buck Mulligan came from the stairhead, bearing a bowl of lather on which a mirror and a razor lay crossed. A yellow dressing-gown, ungirdled, was sustained gently behind him by the mild morning air. He held the bowl aloft and intoned:

—*Introibo ad altare Dei.*

Halted, he peered down the dark winding stairs and called up coarsely:

—Come up, Kinch. Come up, you fearful jesuit.

Solemnly he came forward and mounted the round gunrest. He faced about and blessed gravely thrice the tower, the surrounding country and the awaking mountains. Then, catching sight of Stephen Dedalus, he bent towards him and made rapid crosses in the air, gurgling in his throat and shaking his head. Stephen Dedalus, displeased and sleepy, leaned his arms on the top of the staircase and looked coldly at the shaking gurgling face that blessed him, equine in its length, and at the light untonsured hair, grained and hued like pale oak.

By the fourth grade, I was an altar boy, having committed to memory the prayers of the Latin Mass. Anyone with such an experience would recognize this scene immediately as a parody of the central ceremony of the Catholic liturgy. Buck Mulligan is the priest saying his morning Mass; Stephen Dedalus (nicknamed Kinch) is his altar server. The Latin sentence Buck intones has been recited millions of times over millennia and across the globe: *Introibo ad altare Dei.* "I approach the altar of God."

The movement from the dark stairwell into the tower and open air elevates the scene, the grandeur of creation all around. It would provide a perfect setting for a profoundly religious experience—or, in this case, a shave.

Let's look closely at that first sentence, in which Buck Mulligan carries the holy objects of shaving: a bowl of lather on which a mirror and a razor lay crossed. If Buck is the priest, that bowl of lather substitutes for the chalice that will hold the blood of Christ. How appropriate that the mirror and the razor lay "crossed," as every Mass takes place before a crucifix and is considered a reenactment—not a symbolic imitation—of the saving suffering of Christ.

Consider the implications of those telling objects. The bowl with lather is like half a globe, the bowl of the world that holds the life-giving sea. The mirror offers countless associations: art, which is an imitation of life; but also self-reflection and introversion, leading to narcissism. And what of the razor—the blade, the sword—symbolizing the life of the warrior, at cross-purposes with the mirror, the conflict between the active and contemplative life?

Then there is that garish yellow dressing gown, which is ungirdled, as opposed to the white alb of the priest saying the Mass, which is held fast in the middle with a cincture, or rope, the vestments transformed metaphorically into the "armor of salvation." Joyce also makes sure that Buck, unlike a monk with a ritualized bald spot atop his head, is "untonsured."

The depth and texture of this prose is startling in its complexity but is grounded in a confidence that can only come from the author's deepest understanding of the language and the symbols with which he is playing.

RITUALS AND ICONS

Joyce handles this same store of imagery with less wit and greater delicacy at the end of the final story in *Dubliners,* "The Dead." This much-honored work has, like *The Great Gatsby,* a treasured ending, so elegant and moving that it has been memorized and recited by countless admirers. One of them was a famous professor of cultural studies named James Carey. Jim, a devout but pragmatic Irish Catholic, and I were attending the birthday party of a friend—quite a rowdy affair, as I remember it—during which a knock at the door produced a surprise bagpiper. Late in an evening first fueled then mellowed by beer, Jim, in his distinctive Rhode Island accent, began his recitation. A kind of transporting magic filled the room, as if we had left behind our bodies in Florida and floated toward the Irish Sea:

> The air of the room chilled his shoulders. He stretched himself cautiously along under the sheets and lay down beside his wife. One by one, they were all becoming shades. Better pass boldly into that other world, in the full glory of some passion, than fade and wither dismally with age. He thought of how she who lay beside him had locked in her heart for so many years that image of her lover's eyes when he had told her that he did not wish to live.
>
> Generous tears filled Gabriel's eyes. He had never felt like that himself towards any woman, but he knew that such a feeling must be love. The tears gathered more thickly in his eyes and in the partial darkness he imagined he saw the form of a young man standing under a

dripping tree. Other forms were near. His soul had approached that region where dwell the vast hosts of the dead. He was conscious of, but could not apprehend, their wayward and flickering existence. His own identity was fading out into a grey impalpable world: the solid world itself, which these dead had one time reared and lived in, was dissolving and dwindling.

A few light taps upon the pane made him turn to the window. It had begun to snow again. He watched sleepily the flakes, silver and dark, falling obliquely against the lamplight. The time had come for him to set out on his journey westward. Yes, the newspapers were right: snow was general all over Ireland. It was falling on every part of the dark central plain, on the treeless hills, falling softly upon the Bog of Allen and, farther westward, softly falling into the dark mutinous Shannon waves. It was falling, too, upon every part of the lonely churchyard on the hill where Michael Furey lay buried. It lay thickly drifted on the crooked crosses and headstones, on the spears of the little gate, on the barren thorns. His soul swooned slowly as he heard the snow falling faintly through the universe and faintly falling, like the descent of their last end, upon all the living and the dead.

At a memorial service for Jim Carey, it was my honor to read this passage, a fitting tribute to a scholar who had the soul of a poet. I daresay it might be possible to organize a writing seminar around this passage alone. Its beauty, dramatic depth, and complexity offer many paths of discovery.

But first the context. The story, around fifty pages long, has the feel of a novella. It is Christmastime, and a young couple, the Conroys, attends a holiday party on a cold, snowy evening. The night is full of Irish palaver and debate about country, church, and family. But things change at the sound of an old Irish ballad. The husband, Gabriel, looks up to a staircase, and there, on the landing, is the silhouette of a woman listening intently to the music. To his surprise, it turns out to be his wife, Gretta.

> He stood still in the gloom of the hall, trying to catch the air that the voice was singing and gazing up at his wife. There was a grace and mystery in her attitude as if she were a symbol of something. He asked himself what is a woman standing on the stairs in the shadow, listening to distant music, a symbol of. If he were a painter he would paint her in that attitude. Her blue felt hat would show off the bronze of her hair against the darkness and the dark panels of her skirt would show off the light ones. *Distant Music* he would call the picture if he were a painter.

Gabriel would soon learn the meaning of that song and its melancholy effects upon Gretta. She would reveal to him the story of a young admirer, Michael Furey, a delicate boy of seventeen, who once stood in the rain under a tree in the freezing cold to serenade his darling Gretta. Already in ill health, he would catch his death of cold. The story with its lyrical beauty and eruption of passion and emotion in his wife catches Gabriel off guard. Could his love for Gretta ever compete with that of Michael Furey? It is those thoughts that lead to the story's final three paragraphs, above. This would be a good time to reread them.

Remember how we X-rayed the name Stephen Dedalus and described it as a blend of Christian and Greek mythology? Joyce seems to repeat the pattern with the name Michael Furey. That first name suggests Saint Michael the Archangel, the great warrior angel depicted in countless forms of Christian art. In Greek mythology, a Fury was a kind of warrior as well, a vengeful spirit who often punished the wicked. How odd, then, that Joyce should give this powerful combination of names to a frail, sickly, love-struck boy.

The Catholic iconography suggested by Michael is repeated in the name of the main character, Gabriel. Michael is the warrior angel; Gabriel is the messenger, the bearer of news to Mary that she will become pregnant by the power of the Holy Spirit.

This pattern of sacramental language continues throughout the story's final paragraph. The snow falls throughout Ireland, including upon the graveyard where the long-lost lover lies buried. Notice this language: "It lay thickly drifted on the crooked crosses and headstones, on the spears of the little gate, on the barren thorns." On first reading, there is nothing here but a clear and sparkling image of the graveyard. Just below the surface we see something more: crosses, spears, and thorns are all instruments of Christ's passion and death.

More impressive to me than the Christian symbolism and the way it turns Michael Furey into a martyr for love is the exquisite imagery of falling snow. It comes from the scattered repetition of the word *falling* seven times in a single paragraph. It echoes the soft sound of falling snow from sibilant phrases such as "His soul swooned slowly." It reaches a balanced crescendo in the parallel inversions of "falling softly" and "softly falling" and of "falling faintly" and "faintly falling."

True to his Irish Catholic diction until the end, Joyce concludes this famous passage with a kind of familiar benediction, though it is only snow and not sanctifying grace that falls upon "the living and the dead." It took me a long time to recognize that Joyce had ended his story with the same two words that constitute its title.

WRITING LESSONS

1. When inventing a name for a character, remember you have a range of choices, from the perfectly appropriate (a baseball player named Charlie Spikes) to the coarsely ironic (the vaudeville character named Dr. Kronkite—*krankheit* being the German word for "disease"). By naming the dead young lover Michael Furey, Joyce unleashed a contrasting range of connotations and associations. Why should a frail boy be named after the warrior archangel? Inside such questions, art is created. When you think of a name for your character— Pedro, Isabel, Butch, Constantine, Bruce—ask yourself, "Who else has that name?" and consider the associations.

2. We have all heard advice on the value of unambiguous clarity, using a precise word because of its specific, targeted meaning. But there are those wonderful days when words just won't cooperate, when, to borrow a phrase from Dylan Thomas, they sing out in their chains. The word *forge* is a perfect example. There is nothing fake in the declaration of Stephen Dedalus. He means forge the way a blacksmith means forge, not the way a crook writing a check means

forge. Yet the tension inside this word must be realized and ultimately embraced—by the reader and the writer.

3. Write what you know. Draw from the word hoard you have accumulated. Get the most from the supply of symbolic language, narrative traditions, and myths you have developed from your education, religion, and experience of culture. Be conscious of the diction in your writing—that is, the levels of language used in a harmonic way. Start by making a list of the language clubs you belong to. For me it might include: journalist, scholar, rock musician, movie buff, Roman Catholic (with Jewish relatives). Then think of the language heritage that derives from each hobby, craft, culture, and professional disposition.

4. As we will discover in several texts, there is a huge difference between redundancy, which in writing refers to an unintended and unnecessary repetition, and the kind of creative repetition that marks a rhythm, an echo, or a refrain. That repetition can be clustered, but it also works when scattered throughout a text. It can be subtle, but Joyce shows us the beauty that comes when it is bold, as in the creative variation "falling faintly" and "faintly falling." Be bold.

5

X

X-raying Sylvia Plath

Jolt of Insight

I began reading serious novels, written for adults, when I was about twelve years old. The Hardy Boys gave way to *The Last Hurrah* by Edwin O'Connor, a sophisticated novel of Boston politics and Irish family loyalties. When I finished the book and felt the weight of it in my hand, I knew that my life had been changed forever. I had access to the secrets of the adult world at my fingertips.

I read that book during my eighth-grade English class at Saint Aidan's. For eleven years, from sixth grade through college, I attended all-male Catholic schools. It was a rigorous education and helped me construct a foundation of literacy I continue to build upon. But it had its limitations. Essentially we were white Catholic boys being educated by white Catholic men, many of them celibate.

From 1960 on, not one classmate was a woman. Not one teacher. In all those years of reading and study I can remember only a handful of woman authors (Emily Dickinson, Willa Cather, Rachel Carson) presented as part of the curriculum. It was only when I was in graduate school at a public university that the tide began to turn, when the work of Flannery O'Connor, Joan Didion, and Nora Ephron began to dazzle my mind and enrich my experience.

It may have been in the summer of 1968 at Oxford that I became vaguely aware of a poet named Sylvia Plath. She had been married to Ted Hughes, who would become England's poet laureate. I would come to know her as a brilliant writer and troubled soul, a woman whose mental illness would lead her to suicide in 1963 at the age of thirty. The story of her death was lurid and disturbing: she died of asphyxiation by placing her head in a gas oven. Her legacy includes volumes of great poetry, short stories, extensive journals, and a single scintillating novel called *The Bell Jar*. That such brilliant work could come from such a damaged spirit is one of the literary miracles of the twentieth century.

SHOCKING INTRUSION

Most of the novels discussed in this book I read years ago. Some mysterious force—I'm not kidding—led me to *The Bell Jar*, which I devoured in October of 2014, about a month after I had submitted what I thought was a completed draft of *The Art of X-ray Reading*. By the time I finished Plath's novel, I knew I wanted—needed—to write about it. That feeling came with the first sentence.

> It was a queer, sultry summer, the summer they electro-
> cuted the Rosenbergs, and I didn't know what I was doing
> in New York.

Before I read another word, I felt the need to X-ray that sentence. At twenty-three words, it is a short and memorable
first sentence for a novel, beginning with subject and verb of
the main clause, always an encouraging sign.

"It was a queer, sultry summer…"

I feel a tension between the adjectives *queer* and *sultry.*
The first carries a judgment of distortion, something not
quite right in the air. The second, *sultry,* has the sense of
something physical, hot and humid, but not necessarily
unpleasant, perhaps carrying a sexual connotation, like the
sound of a tenor sax. (I've always felt that individual letters
can carry hidden meanings. It may seem strange to say, but
the letter *u* makes me uneasy, especially that triple dose of it
in the phrase "queer, sultry summer.")

What comes next is a shocking intrusion: "the summer
they electrocuted the Rosenbergs…"

A lot of things happened during the summer of 1953,
when the story takes place: the Korean War ended; JFK and
Jackie were married in Newport, Rhode Island; television
was coming into its own. An obsession with a New York Jewish couple executed for espionage aligns with *queer* and connects the collective paranoia of the McCarthy era with our
protagonist's distorted view of reality.

Each of us brings our autobiography to the reading of
any text, and I confess a lifelong fascination with the Rosenbergs. I took a boyish interest in spying, the Soviet menace,

the FBI, and the atomic bomb. We did have civil defense drills in elementary school in which we practiced hiding under desks with our hands covering our heads to protect ourselves from the Red menace. More particularly, for the first four years of my life, 1948–1952, I lived in an apartment complex on the Lower East Side of New York City called Knickerbocker Village. The Rosenbergs lived there, too. After the Rosenbergs' executions in 1953, my uncle Pete and aunt Millie, who were on a waiting list, got their apartment!

That final clause of that first sentence stands out for its multiple meanings. An actor could read it in different ways:

> I didn't know *what* I was doing in New York.
> I didn't know what I was *doing* in New York.
> I didn't know what I was doing in *New York*.

The whole sentence moves with remarkable efficiency from a season to an era to the confusion of a single young woman.

RAISING THE DEAD

If something is important enough to place in the first sentence of a novel, even as a seeming aside, is it important enough to revisit? We saw in *Gatsby* how the author introduced the green light on Daisy's dock in the first chapter, how he reintroduced that light in the middle of the novel, and how he brought it back, with dozens of suggestive thematic implications, at the end. We come to expect that type of exquisite story architecture from our favorite literary artists.

So beyond my personal curiosity about the Rosenbergs, should I expect them to return to the stage later in Plath's novel? Here is what follows that first sentence:

> I'm stupid about executions. The idea of being electro-cuted makes me sick, and that's all there was to read about in the papers—goggle-eyed headlines staring up at me on every street corner and at the fusty, peanut-smelling mouth of every subway. It had nothing to do with me, but I couldn't help wondering what it would be like, being burned alive all along your nerves.
>
> I thought it must be the worst thing in the world.

"It had nothing to do with me." Yeah, right. It has *everything* to do with our protagonist, Esther Greenwood, a fill-in for Plath in this highly autobiographical novel, who, during an internship at a fashion magazine in New York City, is trau-matized time and again.

Sure enough, the Rosenbergs reappear on page 100 of my edition, the beginning of chapter 9. Esther is speaking with another young woman at the fashion magazine about the imminent execution of Ethel and Julius:

> So I said, "Isn't it awful about the Rosenbergs?"
> The Rosenbergs were to be electrocuted late that night.
> "Yes!" Hilda said, and at last I felt I had touched a human string in the cat's cradle of her heart. It was only as the two of us waited for the others in the tomblike morning gloom of the conference room that Hilda ampli-fied that Yes of hers.

"It's awful such people should be alive.... I'm so glad
they're going to die."

This dispiriting moment comes just before the crisis that
will crush our protagonist at the end of the first half of the
book, when a blind date turns into a muddy rape attempt
that leaves her physically injured and emotionally devas-
tated, so much so that she returns to her hotel and throws all
the glamorous clothes she has accumulated off the top of the
skyscraper.

> Piece by piece, I fed my wardrobe to the night wind, and
> flutteringly, like a loved one's ashes, the gray scraps were
> ferried off, to settle here, there, exactly where I would
> never know, in the dark heart of New York.

In that dark moment, Plath offers a kind of silent conver-
gence of the public and the private. Almost at the exact time
the Rosenbergs would be electrocuted, the main character
undergoes a kind of symbolic death, her clothes being scattered to the winds, "like a loved one's ashes."

LIVING WHAT YOU DREAD

The second half of *The Bell Jar* takes place in Massachusetts:
Esther has returned to her home in a dark cloud of depression. It is a fictionalized version of Plath's own mental and
emotional deterioration, a series of imagined and real suicide
attempts that result in the protagonist's institutionalization.

The rooms, patients, doctors, and therapies are chronicled, building up to one terrible failed attempt to cure her:

> And as Doctor Gordon led me into a bare room at the back of the house, I saw that the windows in that part were indeed barred, and that the room door and the closet door and the drawers of the bureau and everything that opened and shut was fitted with a keyhole so it could be locked up....
>
> Doctor Gordon was fitting two metal plates on either side of my head. He buckled them into place with a strap that dented my forehead, and gave me a wire to bite.
>
> I shut my eyes.
>
> There was a brief silence, like an indrawn breath.
>
> Then something bent down and took hold of me and shook me like the end of the world. Whee-ee-ee-ee-ee, it shrilled, through an air crackling with blue light, and with each flash a great jolt drubbed me till I thought my bones would break and the sap fly out of me like a split plant.
>
> I wondered what terrible thing it was that I had done.

At the end of the novel a more compassionate doctor and a more competent version of shock therapy would result in her return to the outside world and hope for a healthier life. (Sadly, the novel ends more happily than the author's real life did.)

It was only after I had closed the book that I was stunned by the beauty of what Plath had created. It was like looking at daybreak pouring through the rose window of a cathedral. All that business about the Rosenbergs—the constant references not to their execution but to their *electrocution*—turned out to be a prologue to the traumatic events in Esther's life, including a medical procedure in a facility that looks and works like a prison in which she is pinned down and wired up (like the Rosenbergs, no doubt) and shot up with electricity. It is, at least at first, her version of the death penalty.

POETIC PROSE

The adventure in X-raying *The Bell Jar* comes from knowing that the author was a poet writing prose. I often work in a discipline—journalism—in which metaphor is discouraged. Let me rephrase that. Figurative language is not discouraged per se; it's reserved for features and opinion writing rather than for neutral reporting. You can understand why. If I write, "Governor Scott walked across the stage with the bald reptilian confidence of Voldemort's younger brother," I have abandoned straight reportage for something more biased—and fun.

In that sense, the literature of journalism is the opposite of poetry, which uses metaphor and other figures of speech to expand the possibilities of language and vision. It should not surprise us, then, that a daring poet such as Sylvia Plath would carry her associative imagination from poetry into fiction.

To savor her poetic sensibilities, we only have to look at the first stanza of one of her most famous poems, "Daddy":

> You do not do, you do not do
> Any more, black shoe
> In which I have lived like a foot
> For thirty years, poor and white,
> Barely daring to breathe or Achoo.

In her book *Break, Blow, Burn,* critic Camille Paglia describes Plath's dangerous and sensational voice:

> Garish, sarcastic, and profane, "Daddy" is one of the strongest poems ever written by a woman. With driving power of voice, it marries the personal to the political against the violent backdrop of modern history. Like Emily Dickinson, another shy New Englander, Sylvia Plath challenges masculine institutions and satirizes outmoded sexual assumptions. But the energies aroused by "Daddy" ultimately become self-devouring. The poem is so extreme that nothing can be built upon it. Plath has had many imitators, but she may have exhausted her style in creating it.

If this is true for Plath's poetry—that she exhausted the style she created in poetry—I would argue that it is *not* true for her prose. In fact, the figurative language in her novels greatly enriches the experience of the reader and establishes a style for fiction that might have led to many more literary adventures if Plath had lived long enough to take them on.

EMPHATIC METAPHORS

As I was X-raying the novel, I began to notice a particular strategy that Plath favors enough to use as often as two or three times per page, sometimes more. What is exciting about this move is that you can read page after page, chapter after chapter, without noticing it. It does not call attention to itself but always advances the narrative.

If you keep track of the metaphors and similes in *The Bell Jar* (a title that is also a metaphor for a distorted, confining, airless existence), you discover that Plath can begin a sentence with figurative language or stick it in the middle, but her preference is to place it at the end. Any word or phrase placed at the end of a sentence stabs the reader. If that emphatic language happens to be metaphorical, the reader feels the steel twice. The blade goes in. The blade comes out.

Whenever I saw this move in the text, I circled it and wrote the word *move* in the margin. (X-ray readers love to write in margins.) Here is a healthy sample:

• I made out men and women, and boys and girls who must be as young as I, but there was a uniformity to their faces, as if they had lain for a long time on a shelf, out of the sunlight, under siftings of pale, fine dust.

• I tried to smile, but my skin had gone stiff, like parchment.

• Being with Jody and Mark and Cal was beginning to weigh on my nerves, like a dull wooden block on the strings of a piano.

- Underneath, the water was green and semi-opaque as a hunk of quartz.
- Against the khaki-colored sand and the green shore wavelets, his body was bisected for a moment, like a white worm.
- A heavy naughtiness pricked through my veins, irritating and attractive as the hurt of a loose tooth.

These are isolated sentences, taken out of context. Attached to action, these metaphors and similes operate on the reader as verbal exclamation points, bringing to a head—and to our heads—some point of insight. As in, "I poked my head out of the covers and stared over the edge of the bed. Around the overturned enamel tray, a star of thermometer shards glittered, and balls of mercury trembled like celestial dew."

Why celestial dew? Because they will soon come to symbolize her shattered and fluid state:

> I opened my fingers a crack, like a child with a secret, and smiled at the silver globe cupped in my palm. If I dropped it, it would break into a million little replicas of itself, and if I pushed them near each other, they would fuse, without a crack, into one whole again.
>
> I smiled and smiled at the small silver ball.

I love those four hissing *s* words that point to the word *ball* at the end.

Even with its scenes so dark and its protagonist so tortured, *The Bell Jar* is a novel written by an author who plays with language. How can such a depressed and suicidal spirit find a place to play with words? That is a great mystery of art. But play Plath does. At one point in *The Bell Jar,* Esther decides she will write about her own experiences, but in the form of a novel. That creates a kind of hall-of-mirrors effect, since that is exactly what Plath is doing in creating Esther Greenwood. She writes:

> A feeling of tenderness filled my heart. My heroine would be myself, only in disguise. She would be called Elaine. Elaine. I counted the letters on my fingers. There were six letters in Esther, too. It seemed a lucky thing.

I had my X-ray glasses on when I read this. I used my index finger to hold my place so that I could examine the cover and the first name of the author. *S-y-l-v-i-a.* Six letters, just like Esther and Elaine. Not lucky, it occurred to me, but very clever; funny, even — and wise.

WRITING LESSONS

1. Many examples of good writing have a one-two-three quality to them: subject, verb, object. In most cases, you don't want the reader to stop or even pause. My mentor Don Fry calls this effect "steady advance." But there will be exceptions, moments when the writer will intrude on the reader's expectations, even in the middle of a sentence. Call it a bump in the road. Plath achieves this effect with the insertion of the Rosenberg execution inside her first sentence. What if that sentence had been: "It was a queer, sultry summer, and I didn't know what I was doing in New York." Clear and com-

pelling enough, but not brilliant and explosive. Most sentences you write will be A-B-C. If you want to catch the reader off guard, consider A-X-B.

2. Not all allusions are created equal. When an author quotes another author or mentions historical figures (such as the Rosenbergs), he or she embeds one narrative within another. As we've seen with the opening of *The Bell Jar,* an apparent offhand comment becomes a much grander metaphor, taking on new contexts and connotations as the narrative builds up steam. Most coherent texts contain a dominant image—sometimes more than one—that links the parts and accelerates the action.

3. Figurative language—such as metaphor and simile—is more common in some forms of writing than in others. Too much of it in prose can call attention to itself or make the writer sound word-drunk. But done with control, it has the effect of expanding consciousness—especially when it is hardly noticeable. When George Orwell argued that good writing is like a windowpane, he was using a metaphor that is *exactly* like a windowpane, a frame for seeing the world, a boundary that is hardly noticeable.

4. That last word or phrase in a sentence or paragraph gets special attention from the reader—whether the writer intends it to or not. Good writers know that these locations are hot spots and reserve them for the most interesting or important language. Plath doubles down (to use a term from blackjack) by using the ends of sentences as places to insert metaphors and similes. In Plath's case, it is like looking through Orwell's windowpane, then throwing open the window to the cool air.

5. Clever writers sometimes play little tricks they know will delight some of their readers. My old friend Howell Raines, an author and a former editor of the *New York Times*, wrote a profile of a young politician whose father was a famous and powerful senator. He began, "Will the son also rise?" a lead sentence clear enough on its face, but even better if it reminds you of Hemingway, and better yet if it gets you to Ecclesiastes. Even if most readers don't get it, some will, and that makes it worth the effort. Plath plays the six-letter-name trick with Esther, Eileen, and, for those wearing their X-specs, Sylvia. On more than one level the act of writing is, to use a fancy word, ludic. It's a game. A game of language, connection, and meaning. Have some fun, for goodness' sake.

6

X

X-raying Flannery O'Connor
Dragon's Teeth

To me Flannery O'Connor is the Buddy Holly of American literature. There is no disputing her greatness, but you wish you could have read what she would have written had she lived to the age of, say, sixty-nine instead of thirty-nine. Like Alice Munro, O'Connor was a master of the short form. No great long novel became part of her legacy, but more than five hundred pages of short stories (thirty-two in all) stand with the greatest American literature any woman, or man, has ever written.

In this chapter, I will X-ray two of her stories, favorites of mine since graduate school: "A Good Man Is Hard to Find" and "Good Country People." The first is as harsh and violent a narrative as anything written by Cormac McCarthy. The

second is as comedic and self-deprecating as anything delivered by Mark Twain.

My plot description of "Good Man" requires a spoiler
alert, except for this: I've known the ending since 1974, and
every time I read it, the story gets creepier and more unset-
tling, not unlike another story we will X-ray, "The Lottery."
O'Connor's story begins with the sentence "The grandmother
didn't want to go to Florida." Seventeen pages later, that
woman will be executed—by an escaped criminal known
only as the Misfit—with three bullets to the chest. (The
moral, suggested a friend on Twitter, is "Always listen to your
grandmother." Well, as we shall see, not always.)

There is much to recommend in this story for a student
of writing and literature: the wonderful characterizations of
the six members of the grandmother's family and the three
fugitives; the bizarre Gothic geography of southern high-
ways and byways; the familiar Catholic themes of original
sin and why horrible things come to people who mean
no harm. But I'd like to focus on one relentless narrative
strategy that exists through the story. For lack of a better
term, I'll call it planting dragon's teeth. The technique
resides in that exquisite territory between foreshadowing
and foreboding.

HERE IT COMES

Another name for this move is "it's coming." In suspenseful
movies, the "it" can be anything dangerous: shark, monster,
criminal, stalker, rival gang, radioactive cloud, tsunami,
zombie, asteroid, alien bacteria, you name it. But before "it"

comes, we have to prepare the reader or viewer for it, so we plant dragon's teeth along the path of a narrative. Let's define a dragon's tooth as any seed—detail, dialogue, place name—that will sprout into something significant later in the story. When you see a sign for a town named Toombsboro, the author has planted a dragon's tooth.

The engine, or dominant question, of "Good Man" goes like this: "What are the chances that the grandmother and her family will run into the Misfit and his henchmen?" In the real world, the answer is simple: there is a greater chance that they will be hit by lightning or win the lottery. But in story world, the deadly encounter arrives on the Island of Destiny in the Sea of Inevitability. The anticipation of danger begins with a dull feeling in the gut of the reader and is made sharper by a seemingly endless series of vague but troubling signposts (dragon's teeth). As the story builds and builds, the signals become clearer. The paths of these characters must cross, and the victims—in some twisted moral algorithm—have earned their fate.

Before we retrace these portents, let's review the distinction between foreshadowing and foreboding, two strategies that are often conflated. Definitions from *The American Heritage Dictionary* will help:

> Forebode: To create a sense of impending peril or misfortune.
> Foreshadow: To present a hint of what may come.

Classic vampire movies are filled with foreboding: a young couple travels through Transylvania by coach. Day turns into night. A clear sky breaks into a violent storm. An open road leads to a narrow one in a forest. You don't need an anemometer to know you're standing in a hurricane.

Foreshadowing tends to be more subtle and is not confined to drama, tragedy, or horror. It works chillingly, as we will see, at the beginning of "The Lottery," when boys at play stuff their pockets with stones—in early anticipation of the stoning at the end. But it works just as well in the comic fables of *The Canterbury Tales,* when we learn, almost as an aside, that the dainty and fastidious Absolon is a bit squeamish, especially when it comes to farting. That detail will be lost in competition with others until the fateful moment when the mischievous Nicholas and Alison play their windy joke on the clownish cleric.

In most cases, you can feel foreboding while it is happening; but to identify foreshadowing, you may need a second or third reading.

Remarkable in O'Connor's work are the ways in which foreshadowing and foreboding converge and diverge, so you are never certain which chicken will come home to roost. Here, in narrative order, are the story elements—the dragon's teeth—portending that something wicked will this way come.

In the first paragraph we are introduced to the grandmother's son, Bailey, described as "her only boy." This sounds innocent enough but is the kind of thing we say when a mother loses her child to an accident or violence. "The real tragedy is she lost her only boy."

Grandma doesn't want to go to Florida because she prefers "to visit some of her connections in east Tennessee," but she makes up an excuse by exaggerating the danger of an escaped criminal, news she learns from that day's paper: "Here this fellow that calls himself The Misfit is aloose from the Federal Pen and headed toward Florida and you read here what it says he did to these people." (What he did is never specified, but is repeated, no doubt, in the climactic violence against the grandmother and her family.)

By the bottom of the first page, we are shown her grandchildren, John Wesley and June Star, odd kids who sass their grandmother in shrill and disrespectful ways. Children do not deserve to die because they sass their elders, of course, but there is a narrative tradition in horror stories that certain kinds of characters — the proud, promiscuous, or disrespectful — eventually get what's coming to them.

O'CONNOR'S CAT

By the second page, Grandma is "the first one in the car, ready to go." She has a big black valise with her, which hides a basket containing the family cat, named Pitty Sing. Her reason: "she was afraid he might brush against one of the gas burners and accidentally asphyxiate himself." It's a tangential reference to accident and death, but in the end it comes to mean something more. O'Connor's cat is a version of the narrative device known as Chekhov's gun. The concept is simple — an author should not put a rifle over the mantel unless a character will think about firing it. You shouldn't put a cat in the backseat of a car unless your plan is to have that cat jump out at a most inopportune moment.

The grandchildren become more obnoxious, declaring

that their home state of Georgia is "lousy." Granny scolds them, but in the process reveals herself: "In my time...children were more respectful of their native states and their parents and everything else. People did right then. Oh look at the cute little pickaninny!" Grandma has seen a small black child standing in the door of a shack and thinks the image would make a nice picture. O'Connor is not the first author to juxtapose two things that reveal a contradiction in character. Chaucer introduces us in *The Canterbury Tales* to the delicate and elegant Prioress, who tells one of the bloodiest and most vicious tales in the cycle. Grandma scolds the children for their disrespect only to immediately reveal her own racism and insensitivity.

"They passed a large cotton field with five or six graves fenced in the middle of it, like a small island." We are still only three pages into the story, but here we are, with husband, wife, grandmother, and three children (including a baby)—six human beings riding in a car—passing a cemetery with "five or six graves." That detail may not sink in on the first read, but on subsequent readings it feels like a morbid foreshadowing.

More misbehavior by the children follows, along with a racist joke about watermelons, more evidence that readers should hold these characters at arm's length. About halfway through the car ride there is a stop at a barbecue joint called the Tower, run by a man named Red Sammy Butts. A conversation ensues in which Red Sammy and grandmother explore the dimensions of their limited moral universe. Grandmother brings up the escaped Misfit. She calls Red Sammy "a good man."

"'A good man is hard to find,' Red Sammy said. 'Everything is getting terrible. I remember the day you could go off and leave your screen door unlatched. Not no more.'" Of course, the title of the story is exposed here (or we could say this dialogue became the title of the story). In the twisted logic of the story, we can invert key elements. If a good man is hard to find, we might presume that a bad man is easy to find. Or to make real the grandmother's premonitions, it is easy for a bad man to find you.

The family continues the trip until they near a town named Toombsboro (the name of an actual small town, spelled without the *b*, in Georgia). Don't let that extra *o* fool you. We've gone from six graves to a tomb. Grandmother suddenly remembers that there is a famous plantation nearby, and a noisy argument ensues about whether or not they should take a detour to see it. The father grudgingly agrees. "'All right,' Bailey said, 'but get this: this is the only time we're going to stop for anything like this.'" How right he turns out to be.

What follows is the narrative equivalent of a Rube Goldberg contraption: as they wind down a road, the grandmother is shocked by a sudden memory; she knocks against her valise; the basket underneath is uncovered; the cat springs onto the driver's shoulder; he swerves the car into a ditch. The memory turns out to be that the plantation she remembered, the one that caused the detour that led to the crash, was not in Georgia but in Tennessee—the place she really wanted to visit. "We've had an ACCIDENT!" the children scream, and it is worth focusing our X-ray vision on that word, which O'Connor places in capital letters. On the common level, the word refers to an unexpected daily occurrence, often related to physical injury or destruction of property. On the metaphysical level, the word *accident* is often used as the opposite of words like *fate, destiny,* and *providence.* O'Connor was steeped in Catholic theology, so it's clear what she's getting at: What kind of universe do we live in? Would a kind and merciful deity steer a family toward disaster?

The grandmother waves at a passing car to help them. "It was a big black battered hearse-like automobile." Of course it was. The three men in that car become the family's executioners.

I have interviewed many writers, including authors of novels. The writers of fiction seem to fall into two categories. The first group might be called the careful planners, writers who sketch out the architecture of a plot before the first draft begins. The second group comprises the plungers. They can see ahead, but just enough to keep going. E. L. Doctorow compared it to driving at night with the headlights on. Those lights let you see down the road apiece, just enough to maintain your forward progress. It would appear from all the clues planted by O'Connor that she might work from a detailed map, but it need not be that way. An early draft can take you from beginning to a gruesome end, which then gives you the opportunity to add telling details during revision, such as the number of graves in a cemetery or the name Toombsboro.

I taught this story to a group of English teachers not long ago and learned an important lesson along the way. When I called attention to the name of the grandmother's cat, Pitty

Sing, I expressed the opinion that it was an odd and silly name. One teacher took the initiative and looked it up on her cell phone. Turns out Pitti-Sing (spelled with an *i*) is one of the names of a minor character in the Gilbert and Sullivan operetta *The Mikado*. Pitti-Sing is the ward of the lord high executioner of a crazy land that is meant as a satirical image of England. At the end of O'Connor's story, Pitty Sing the cat is a survivor and becomes, in his own way, the ward of an executioner, the Misfit. Moral of the story, writers: always look it up.

Despite differences in tone and theme, it would not be hard to guess that the author of "A Good Man Is Hard to Find" also wrote "Good Country People." The second story is as hilarious as the first is horrifying. But other elements are familiar: the culture of the southern countryside, the authentic feel for rural speech patterns, the interesting blend among characters of familiar and bizarre. The channels may be different, but the voices sound as if they are coming through the same radio.

For our purposes, though, there is one great difference visible through our X-ray glasses. In "Good Man," we see countless signs that the climax of the story, however shocking, seems inevitable. In "Good Country People" the outcome may feel like a form of poetic justice, but it comes as a jolt, almost like a punch line.

In short, a woman living with her mother in rural Georgia meets a young traveling salesman. The woman has a PhD in philosophy and a wooden leg, the result of a hunting accident in childhood. He sells Bibles. She arranges a meeting with him on the outskirts of the property, near a hay barn, hoping to seduce him. They kiss and embrace in the hayloft. He persuades her to take off her leg, which he proceeds to steal. Turns out he wasn't "good country people" after all but a fetishist and a pervert. Believe it or not, I'm leaving out the good parts.

NAME GAME

Before we get to the good parts, I would be remiss not to call attention to the characters' names. Our protagonist is named Joy Hopewell by her optimistic mother but goes off to college and changes her first name to Hulga.

"Mrs. Hopewell [the mother] was certain that she had thought and thought until she had hit upon the ugliest name in any language. Then she had gone and had the beautiful name, Joy, changed without telling her mother until after she had done it. Her legal name was Hulga."

To emphasize the ugliness of the name, O'Connor plays a wonderful game with the reader. It works like this and may be invisible without your X-ray glasses: every mention of her new name is followed either by alliteration or assonance, especially the repetition of the ugly *u* sound. Some examples (the italics are mine):

• When Mrs. Hopewell thought the name, Hulga, she thought of the broad blank *hull* of a battleship.

• She had a vision of the name working like the *ugly* sweating *Vulcan* who stayed in the furnace...

• When Hulga *stumped* into the kitchen...

The name game doesn't stop there. The tenant farmers are called the Freemans. Their daughters are named Glynese and Carramae. "Joy called them Glycerin and Caramel." And then there is the name of the Bible salesman, something pulled from a *Playboy* cartoon or Restoration comedy: Manley Pointer.

TWEAKING STORY FORMS

The first time I read "Good Country People" it felt as if I were listening to a familiar old joke. "There was this traveling salesman who knocked on the door of a farmhouse. The door opened and inside was a farmer, his wife, and his beautiful daughter." In most versions of this narrative, the salesman outwits the farmer and beds the naive but desirable daughter.

Consider O'Connor's manipulation of the stock characters and standard elements. Rather than making the daughter a voluptuous Daisy Duke or Elly May Clampett or Daisy Mae Scragg, she is Hulga, an atheist philosopher with a PhD and a wooden leg. Her hubris is that she sees herself as worldly and sophisticated in comparison to Manley Pointer, whom she looks down upon as green.

The inversion plays out as the salesman carries his case of Bibles up into the hayloft. As the seduction unwinds, it becomes clear who is in control:

> He leaned the other way and pulled the valise toward him and opened it. It had a pale blue spotted lining and there were only two Bibles in it. He took one of these out and

opened the cover of it. It was hollow and contained a pocket flask of whiskey, a pack of cards, and a small blue box with printing on it. He laid these out in front of her one at a time in an evenly-spaced row, like one presenting offerings at the shrine of a goddess. He put the blue box in her hand. THIS PRODUCT TO BE USED ONLY FOR THE PREVENTION OF DISEASE, she read, and dropped it. The boy was unscrewing the top of the flask. He stopped and pointed, with a smile, to the deck of cards. It was not an ordinary deck but one with an obscene picture on the back of each card. "Take a swig," he said, offering her the bottle first. He held it in front of her, but like one mesmerized, she did not move.

The details are ingenious. What better emblem for hypocrisy than a hollow Bible? In that container are the sacramentals of sin: condoms, booze, porn. He leaves just enough room in his valise to abscond with her wooden leg, another trophy of his bizarre conquest. "One time I got a woman's glass eye this way."

WRITING LESSONS

1. To combine foreboding and foreshadowing, plant dragon's teeth along the path of the story. A dragon's tooth is any narrative seed that bears fruit toward the end. Make sure you vary them and spread them out across the story.

2. Remember that most readers will experience foreboding in real time, as the story is being read. To experience foreshadowing may require multiple readings. On a second

reading, the reader should be able to recognize these hints, leading perhaps to some inevitable conclusion.

3. Play with personal names and place names to differentiate characters, but also use them to reveal a virtue or vice in a particular character. Remember that the "good man" in O'Connor's story is named Red Sammy Butts.

4. When inspired by stereotypes or stock characters, such as traveling salesmen and farmers' daughters, you may have to balance two contradictory goals: to satisfy the requirements of a pattern and to surprise the reader with variations from the norm.

5. Find physical objects, or what Tom Wolfe describes as "status details," that represent traits of character or reveal strengths and weaknesses, such as the hollow Bible, an emblem of the salesman's hypocrisy. As Hulga dresses for her seduction, O'Connor notes, "She wore a pair of slacks and a dirty white shirt, and as an afterthought, she had put some Vapex on the collar of it since she did not own any perfume." That she would use a mentholated ointment to stand in for perfume says much about Hulga's economic status and lack of romantic sophistication.

7

X

X-raying "The Lottery"

Piling Stones

Shirley Jackson once said she wrote the short story "The Lottery" in one sitting, and I believe her. On June 26, 1948, soon after it was written, it was published in *The New Yorker* magazine, and it may have been the first serious story that ever moved me. Wait. "Moved me" is a euphemism. It scared the shit out of me. Among Jackson's talents as a writer was her ability to evoke terror, as exhibited in her 1959 novel, *The Haunting of Hill House,* widely considered to be among the best haunted house novels ever written.

I encountered "The Lottery" in an anthology in the early 1960s, when I was in high school. The first thing I might have noticed was its brevity, a relief from longer assignments. The story was just ten book pages long, so quick and sharp it felt like a knife in the back. It's hard to think of a shorter story that has been so widely read and remarkably influential.

But before fame came infamy. Upon publication, "The Lottery" soon generated more mail than any work of fiction in the history of *The New Yorker,* the great majority of the letters expressing puzzlement, disgust, or outrage. So much hostile mail filled Shirley Jackson's Vermont mailbox that she would write about the experience in the essay "Biography of a Story." The problem for many readers was a failure to recognize the story as a work of fiction. They thought "The Lottery" was real.

In other words, they thought there was a small rural village somewhere in America—in New England, perhaps—where a fertility ritual was held every summer. An old black box was carted out of storage into the town square. The names of family members were placed in the box. And when everyone was present, a family name, then the name of a single individual, was drawn. The winner of the lottery was stoned to death.

In case you skipped over that last sentence, I'll repeat it, and put it in italics. *The winner of the lottery was stoned to death.* Jackson blamed reader misperception upon ignorance, but that was too harsh. Let's remember that a decade earlier, in 1938, some panic erupted over a fictional radio broadcast, *The War of the Worlds* by Orson Welles, in which Earth was under invasion by aliens from Mars. Nor can we forget that the 1940s saw the Holocaust, the genocidal extermination of Jews and others in Nazi concentration camps. With such scapegoating on a massive scale, the ritual execution of a single woman may not have seemed so unimaginable. It's hard to think of rank-and-file readers of a magazine as sophisticated as *The New Yorker* as ignorant or simpleminded.

The source of confusion, I now believe, is the way the story was written. Readers thought "The Lottery" was real because Shirley Jackson created a world that seemed real. How she did that, and how we can do that, will be revealed in our X-ray reading.

To summarize again, the story is set in a small rural town that each summer conducts a lottery. If the lottery goes well, tradition dictates, a good crop will follow. The town's three hundred or so people gather in the town square and draw pieces of paper out of an old black box. What Shirley Jackson leaves for the very end of the story, with taut suspense, is the nature of the "prize" for the winner of the lottery, in this case a Mrs. Tessie Hutchinson. Here is the chilling conclusion:

> Bill Hutchinson went over to his wife and forced the slip of paper out of her hand. It had a black spot on it, the black spot Mr. Summers had made the night before with the heavy pencil in the coal-company office. Bill Hutchinson held it up, and there was a stir in the crowd.
>
> "All right, folks," Mr. Summers said. "Let's finish quickly."
>
> Although the villagers had forgotten the ritual and lost the original black box, they still remembered to use stones. The pile of stones the boys had made earlier was ready; there were stones on the ground with the blowing scraps of paper that had come out of the box.

Mrs. Delacroix selected a stone so large she had to pick it up with both hands and turned to Mrs. Dunbar. "Come on," she said. "Hurry up."

Mrs. Dunbar had small stones in both hands, and she said, gasping for breath, "I can't run at all. You'll have to go ahead and I'll catch up with you."

The children had stones already, and someone gave little Davy Hutchinson a few pebbles.

Tessie Hutchinson was in the center of a cleared space by now, and she held her hands out desperately as the villagers moved in on her. "It isn't fair," she said. A stone hit her on the side of the head.

Old Man Warner was saying, "Come on, come on, everyone." Steve Adams was in the front of the crowd of villagers, with Mrs. Graves beside him.

"It isn't fair, it isn't right," Mrs. Hutchinson screamed, and then they were upon her.

Let's examine how this final scene unfolds, focusing on strategies most storytellers can use.

CALL THE TOWNSPEOPLE TOGETHER

When my mom was a daily watcher of TV soap operas, she often commented on how those stories were organized. "Watch for the party scenes," she'd say. "Especially the weddings." It was at such social events that the various characters, subplots, and narrative threads could be joined together. That insight applies to storytelling in every form I can think of. Chaucer gathers twenty-nine pilgrims at the

Tabard Inn at the beginning of *The Canterbury Tales.* As the frame for *The Decameron,* Boccaccio gathers seven women and three men in a villa outside Florence, where they seek shelter from the Black Death. Consider how Shakespeare gathers most of the main characters in *Hamlet* to attend the play within the play—"The Mousetrap"—in which the king's treachery will be revealed. As we shall see in some detail, King Arthur gathers his courtiers for a huge Christmas party at the beginning of *Sir Gawain and the Green Knight. The Godfather* begins at the wedding of the don's daughter—and ends with a christening (while mobsters gun down their rivals). The second season of *Buffy the Vampire Slayer* ends splendidly with an apocalyptic battle at a high school graduation. And think of how Frank Capra— about the same time Jackson was writing her story—was persuading moviegoers that this is *A Wonderful Life* in the final scene, in which the townspeople squeeze into George Bailey's living room, donate money to pay his debt, drink, and sing Christmas carols.

It is quite remarkable that Jackson could pull off this trick of gathering in so few pages. We learn early on that the whole process of the lottery in this town is conducted within two hours. That gives the story the feel of the classical unities—time, place, and action. But time does pass and the town square fills, at first gradually and innocently enough— with schoolchildren—and then with more urgency.

There is communal terror here—the sacrificial taking of a life, with the blind compliance of all the citizens. Look at the characters who are brought in to carry out the sentence. They begin with the scapegoat's husband, then Mr. Summers, then two women, then the little son, then Old Man Warner, then a young man in front of a crowd next to a woman with the last name Graves. These individuals are not chosen for their distinctive identities. They are differentiated only to reveal that their differences in age, strength, and association are overcome by the communal fear and hatred that turns them all into ritual killers.

STONES TO PEBBLES

To understand the narrative efficiency in "The Lottery," we have to understand the difference between the words *stone* and *rock,* and this requires that we don our X-ray glasses. Dictionaries reveal that in most circumstances the two words are used as synonyms. I can say that I threw a rock through my neighbor's window, or that I threw a stone, and no reader would wonder about the difference.

I could find no instance in the story where Jackson uses the word *rock* for variation. It's stones, stones, and more stones. Consider this early passage:

> Bobby Martin had already stuffed his pockets full of stones, and the other boys soon followed his example, selecting the smoothest and roundest stones; Bobby and Harry Jones and Dickie Delacroix...eventually made a great pile of stones in one corner of the square and guarded it against the raids of the other boys.

In the next paragraph, stones will be mentioned twice more. In the passage leading up to the ritual execution of

Mrs. Hutchinson, the word *stone* or *stones* is repeated seven times. (The only variation is not *rocks* but *pebbles,* which are placed into the hand of little Davy Hutchinson for use against his mother. This is a brilliant and poignant choice by Jackson, a reminder of how we train our children to carry on our culture's darkest practices.)

Stone is the word of choice for Jackson because it's a name for a form of execution — stoning — an ancient practice in many cultures and religions that, however barbaric, can still be found today. It has long been a punishment for women and men caught in adultery. The benefit of stoning — if there can be one — is that it's a communal activity. In the absence of a professional executioner, no one knows for sure who has dealt the fatal blow. Given the theme of "The Lottery" — the blindness of communities locked into mindless traditions — stoning turns out to be the perfect choice.

Since I have read the story so many times now, it is almost impossible for me to identify the places where as reader I begin to worry about the outcome. In some stories, foreshadowing is obvious; in better stories it may not be recognizable at first glance. In other words, you may have to experience the story more than once to get the connection. So it was at the beginning of "The Lottery." Those piles of stones looked like the makings of a childish game rather than implements of ritual murder. Each mention of the word *stone* becomes the percussive beat of a death march.

A DARK AND SUNNY NIGHT

Nothing in the first paragraph of "The Lottery" should cause concern in the reader. The weather is "clear and sunny," flowers are blossoming, and the grass is thick and green. On this beautiful day people are gathering in the square. The lottery will take less than two hours, which is a good thing, so that villagers will be able "to get home for noon dinner." (Hmm. Let's stone the lady to death and go home and eat some fried chicken!)

Readers imagine that an important clue to the tone and action of a story will be its setting, which includes descriptions of the weather. An X-ray reading of "The Lottery" reminds us that nature is oblivious to the moods and needs of human beings. I can remember a terrible day in the history of my family when the Florida sun was shining and a balmy breeze made it seem like paradise. September 11, 2001, was a sparkling day in New York City until the planes hit the towers. We were all brought up on scary stories that occurred on dark and stormy nights. We may be tempted to harmonize nature with narrative action and emotion. This is usually a mistake. Weather can alter human action, of course. But for better or worse, nature is indifferent.

When exactly, then, might a reader feel uneasy? Perhaps when the men gather and we read that "their jokes were quiet and they smiled rather than laughed." I admit to being hyperattentive to language, but that distinction—smiling rather than laughing—suggests a hint of anxiety and self-consciousness. The tone of the story turns darker when the black box is carted out. Jackson makes a lot out of the appearance of the box. Not only is it black, it's also shabby and splintered. When not in use, it is moved from place to place for storage. We learn that there had once been a ritual associated with the lottery, a "tuneless chant" and some kind of "salute." Then there is some gossip about how the lottery had been eliminated in some villages. This negative energy builds and builds until the "winner" of the lottery utters her complaints about the unfairness of it all... "and then they were upon her."

Death at the end has become a pattern. We've seen the murder at the end of *Gatsby;* murder at the end of *Lolita;* death of mother and child by way of Hemingway; six murders at the end of "A Good Man Is Hard to Find"; and a ritual execution to end "The Lottery." Whatever our hopes and dreams, we cannot escape the fact that stories are largely about the suffering — and occasionally the deaths — of sympathetic characters.

BLESSING BECOMES A CURSE

One of the most persistent narrative patterns in literature, including journalism, is the manner in which a curse can become a blessing and a blessing can become a curse. In most nonfiction stories about lotteries that I know, the winner gets a lot of money and then squanders it, falling into depression and regret. A Florida man was murdered for his winnings. That pattern is played out in "The Lottery" and imitated in *The Hunger Games* and its sequels, a series of popular novels and movies about a young woman who must fight to the death against other "winners" of a lottery, in this case a ritual of state control. In many cases in which you are chosen for something, you might win a prize. In the case of gambling, you might "hit your number." But also consider the idiom "Your number is up." Perhaps you were chosen in the military draft or for jury duty or the graveyard shift. In each case, random chance can collide with human choice to create destiny. A blessing—such as becoming Princess Diana—can become a curse. And a curse—such as breaking your ankle—can become a blessing when you marry the nurse.

WRITING LESSONS

1. Gather the townspeople. Most characters in stories interact one-on-one or in small groups. Look for opportunities to bring them together, especially in the middle of narratives, where we can take stock of them. Many of the opportunities for such gatherings are ritualistic, such as weddings and funerals, which lend their own energy to the larger narrative.

2. Differentiate between synonyms. Remember that Jackson repeated *stones* and did not allow any variation for *rock*. There is value in not accidentally repeating a key word. When you do repeat one, do so purposefully, squeezing every ounce of meaning out of it. When you repeat and repeat, and *then* vary, as when Jackson mentions the pebbles in the hand of the young boy, it will magnify the effect.

3. Nature need not cooperate and often should not. To create an appropriate setting and landscape for a story, the weather has to do something, but it need not align itself with

the will of human beings. Happy times can occur in blizzards. The sun smiles down on bloody killers. The more realistic your work, the more unpredictable the connection between the elements outside and the internal landscape of character and motive.

4. Tie the ending to the beginning. We are seeing a recurrence of this pattern, in which a story seems to return to the place where it began. The narrator of *Gatsby* sees that green light on Daisy's dock at the beginning and at the end. Grandma in "Good Man" reads about the Misfit at the beginning of the story and meets him at the end. The stones piled up by children at the beginning of "The Lottery" kill Mrs. Hutchinson at the end. The key is this: even though a pattern is repeated or a character returns, nothing is as it was the first time.

5. Reveal how a blessing becomes a curse. Blessings and curses rotate in a kind of yin-yang wheel until it is hard to recognize the distinction. This pattern exists, of course, in real life, made emblematic in the phrase "Be careful what you wish for." It occurs in every dimension of narrative and myth, from creation stories to beast fables to nursery rhymes. When a character or a circumstance appears too good, warns editor Mike Wilson, look for "the bruise on the apple."

6. Kill someone at the end. Go ahead: pull the trigger, light the fuse, reveal the dagger hidden in the desk drawer. One of the two dominant modes of dramatic narrative — tragedy — requires suffering and, ultimately, death. But death can work in comedy as well, as a prologue to the birth of a new generation.

8

X

X-raying *Madame Bovary*
Signs of Inner Life

I am not fluent in French, but I can read it thanks to a couple of years of college study. If I were an expert in French rather than English, Gustave Flaubert might rank as my favorite writer. (Sorry, Willie Shakespeare, but old Gus might have been one of your favorite writers, too. I could imagine you adapting *Madame Bovary* for the stage.)

I've reread that classic French novel in an able translation by Lowell Bair. And I've revisited commentary on the book by a critic I learned to admire early in my career as a scholar. His name is Erich Auerbach, and his 1953 book *Mimesis: The Representation of Reality in Western Literature* endures as a worthy classic of twentieth-century modernist criticism.

It turns out that Auerbach is an excellent X-ray reader. In

helping us understand how an artist like Flaubert represented or imitated reality (the word *mimesis* is Greek for "imitation"), he offers writers, at least indirectly, advice on how we, too, can undertake one of the most important literary tasks, whether in fiction or nonfiction: to hold up a mirror to the world and create a convincing version that readers can enter.

If you have yet to read *Madame Bovary,* please put it on your list. Emma is a great character, a true romantic, sensuous and sentimental but also ambitious, seeking escape from the suffocating routines of provincial France. She finds a devoted husband, Charles. He is a doctor, but ordinary, narrow-minded, oafish, and lacking the dashing spirit Emma so desperately desires. She tries to break away, but her rebellion leads to her tragic decline—her suffering and death being the inevitable outcomes.

Flaubert captures his heroine's ennui in a nutshell:

> But it was especially at mealtimes that she felt she could bear her life no longer, in that little room on the ground floor with its smoking stove, squeaking door, sweating walls and damp stone floor. All the bitterness of life seemed to be served up to her on her plate, and as the steam rose from the boiled meat, waves of nausea rose from the depths of her soul. Charles was a slow eater; she would nibble a few hazelnuts, or lean on her elbow and idly make lines in the oilcloth with her knife.

Before I share some of Auerbach's X-ray insights, let me offer a few of my own. I begin with a strategic question that many writers must answer: How do you generate interest and energy by describing a moment in time when nothing seems to be happening? That is the case here. If we sat at that table with Charles and Emma, it would appear—at the level of our senses—that nothing of significance was occurring.

This, sadly, too often reflects our daily lives. I am on the couch watching a baseball game, my feet up, eating a slice of reheated pizza and drinking a Coke, while my wife sits beside me knitting a baby blanket. Our cat, Willow, sits between us. This is a moment that might be going on in a thousand households. Domestic routine. Yet who knows what simmers beneath the surface? I am now making this up: maybe she worries about me or is angry with me because I sit around all weekend watching sports and eating junk food. She eats good food and goes to yoga class four days a week. She tries to cook healthful meals for the family, while I prefer a bag of white powdered doughnuts and a glass of chocolate milk. So she really loves me and cares about me and wants me to lead a long life. Or maybe she has her eye on that neighbor down the street who jogs with his shirt off, and maybe she wishes her husband could be more like him. Or maybe the man sitting beside her is her meal ticket, the one whose work has provided her with a standard of living she enjoys, and that is what she doesn't want to lose.

The external details of our lives can sometimes mask the turmoil that constitutes our inner selves. But they can offer clues as to the tempests inside. That's the trick Flaubert executes with consummate skill in this passage. And that's what we should be striving for in our own writing.

DETAILS OF DESPERATION

Let's begin with that first clause, which feels, even in a narrative context, like a traditional thesis statement in a paragraph: "But it was especially at mealtimes that she felt she could bear her life no longer...." That is a powerful statement of negation, desperation, perhaps suicide, and it leads us to a search for evidence: What, in fact, could she be experiencing that is so destructive it would lead her to abandon hope? It should not escape us that Flaubert locates such desperation "at mealtimes." Think of the good associations meals have: nourishment, family, celebration, community, holy communion. But we also know from common experience how such moments of coming together can bring out the worst in married couples and extended families.

What are the sources of such hopelessness? The room begins to talk to Emma and to readers: "in that little room on the ground floor with its smoking stove, squeaking door, sweating walls and damp stone floor." Every word carries meaning: she dreams of mansions, we learn, but the room is little; she imagines towers and balconies overlooking gorgeous landscapes, but she lives on the ground floor. Each part of the room seems noxious, attacking and irritating rather than satisfying the senses. The stove smokes, the door squeaks, the walls sweat, and the floor is cold and damp.

It's worth noting here that the translator inverts the order of the elements from Flaubert's original. In French it reads: "avec le poêle qui fumait, la porte qui criait, les murs qui suintaient, les pavés humides," literally, "with the stove that smokes, the door that squeaks, the walls that sweat, the floor [that is] damp." The original—except for that last phrase, which ends with *humides*—derives meaning from verbs, not adjectives. It's as if each element in the room is an agent assigned to drive Emma to madness.

BITTERNESS ON A PLATE

In the second sentence, Flaubert makes a common move for writers. Using both literal and metaphoric language, he guides the reader up and down the ladder of abstraction— between language that expresses specific things and language that expresses ideas. He begins with "All the bitterness of life seemed to be served up to her on her plate." Notice the quick move between the painful abstraction "the bitterness of life" (in French it's rendered more painful as the bitterness of "l'existence") and the idea of it being served on a plate, which might seem like a cliché if it were not taking place at the dinner table.

Then comes "and as the steam rose from the boiled meat, waves of nausea rose from the depths of her soul." As in the earlier litany of kitchen irritants, Flaubert makes use of parallel constructions, in this case to match opposites. As the steam rises from the meat, nausea rises from her soul. It's not as parallel in the French, and the translator has again inverted the author's original order, which places a final emphasis in the sentence not on soul but rather on the feelings of nausea. The meal, which should be nurturing, provokes only metaphysical and emotional dyspepsia. Pass the Alma Seltzer. Or the Pepto Abysmal.

SMALL GESTURES FILLED WITH MEANING

Charles does not enter the picture until the third sentence, where he rates only a few words: "Charles was a slow eater." That description says nothing about his character out of the context of Emma's frustration. When something is boring or painful, we pray that it will pass quickly. As he eats so slowly, Emma is trapped in her thoughts and idle gestures: "she would nibble a few hazelnuts, or lean on her elbow and idly make lines in the oilcloth with her knife." I was fascinated by the balance in this part of the sentence between the nibbling of the nuts and the idle handling of the knife. There is a sense of danger, to be sure—to herself, perhaps to others—an existential angst that might anticipate the work of a French writer of the twentieth century, Jean-Paul Sartre. The titles of some of his works—*Nausea* and *No Exit*—could easily apply to Emma Bovary.

But once again, I see a slightly different emphasis in the French of Flaubert and the English of his translator. Flaubert did not save "knife" (*couteau*) for the final emphatic word. A literal translation of the French original would go something like this: "With the point of a knife she amuses herself by poking at the surface of the oilcloth [*la toile cirée*]." The emphasis at the end falls on her stabbing the oilcloth—the cheap covering over the table. Most crucial is what is not there: an expensive tablecloth she would own in the life she imagines.

MYSTERY OF MOTIVE

Let's examine what Erich Auerbach sees beneath this pas-sage: "The paragraph itself presents a picture — man and wife together at mealtime. But the picture is not presented in and for itself; it is subordinated to the dominant subject, Emma's despair."

That much is clear, and it represents the kind of insight a critic makes when he is describing the theme of a literary work. It's about despair, we say, the way we say that *Othello* is about jealousy. Discussion of theme in literature is meant to be expansive but often limits our choices and our vision of the work, for a masterpiece such as *Othello* turns out to be about many things. As is *Madame Bovary.*

I am tempted to argue that what makes Shakespeare's work superior to Flaubert's — however great — is what Har-vard scholar Stephen Greenblatt describes as the "opacity of motive." The theory is that the *less* we know about someone's motive (such as Iago's), or the greater the complexity of the motive (such as Hamlet's), the greater the work of art.

In *Othello,* for example, we know that Shakespeare drew upon an earlier version of the story in which the motives of Iago were clear. In the source, Iago plays his vengeful trick upon Othello, resulting in the murder of Desdemona out of anger and jealousy. He is in love with Desdemona himself, but she doesn't see it. Shakespeare's version removes that motive and replaces it with — nothing. Remember Iago's chilling final words: "Demand me nothing. What you know, you know. From this time forth I never will speak word."

While readers want an answer to the question of why,

the work is often better if a character's motivations remain cloudy. Emma's motivations are not opaque, but they are complex, and they feel as real as that knife on the tablecloth. That complexity should remind writers to avoid the logical fallacy of the single cause: that the mass killer did what he did because of "mental illness," or "easy access to guns," or "the influence of violent video games." In fiction, the complexity of motive adds texture to a work and mystery and intrigue to the experience of reading.

ARROW OF INDIRECTION

Auerbach has stated something obvious—that the subject of Flaubert's story is Emma's despair. More helpful is the critic's sense of *how* the author communicates that feeling or message. He argues that Flaubert does this through indirection—not through the expression of opinion but through a description of Emma's experience, internal and external:

> We hear the writer speak; but he expresses no opinion and makes no comment. His role is limited to selecting the events and translating them into language; and this is done in the conviction that every event, if one is able to express it purely and completely, interprets itself and the persons involved in it far better and more completely than any opinion or judgment appended to it could do. Upon this conviction—that is, upon a profound faith in the truth of language responsibly, candidly, and carefully employed—Flaubert's artistic practice rests.

That the author's opinion may be unspoken does not mean that he lacks an opinion. It does mean that he or she expresses ideas and feelings—especially related to character—indirectly. One version of this writing technique comes from the old school: show, don't tell. (Although we must respect Francine Prose's warning that not every emotion in a narrative needs to be acted out.) I prefer the advice from the late journalist and author Richard Ben Cramer, who wrote masterfully about politics and sports. He once told me that he measured his research by its ability to lead him to a clear, dominant feeling concerning the person he was writing about, be it Jerry Lee Lewis, Bob Dole, or Joe DiMaggio. He then asked himself: "What led me to feel that way?" In search of an answer, he reexamined the most convincing evidence. His final job was to present that evidence to the reader in the form of scenes, dialogue, character details, and anecdotes. The idea was to create a vicarious experience for the reader, one that would guide the reader toward the same dominant feeling, knowing full well that no writer can control a reader's reaction to the work.

WRITING LESSONS

1. Look for the smallest domestic details that reveal the complexities of a character's inner life. Those complexities will almost always include the negative, problematic, or painful feelings of existence, the crosses we bear, the steps we regret.

2. What the characters are *not* doing is as important, and sometimes more important, than their direct actions

and reveals aspects of their histories and personalities. Emma's passivity in the kitchen, marked by tiny, futile gestures, speaks more loudly than crashed dishes on the floor.

3. In the absence of action by the characters, some force must step in and replace it. This includes inanimate objects. A door can act. Or a wall. Or a plate. Or something on the plate. All this and more is happening in Flaubert's passage.

4. Given the choice between a word in adjective or verb form, opt for the verb, which tends to be stronger. I prefer Flaubert's original phrasing to that of his translator. A door that squeaks speaks louder than a squeaking door. This effect can be enhanced by parallel constructions, used sometimes to compare equal elements and sometimes to contrast them.

5. Use the routine setting to generate metaphors—in this case the plate, which holds unpalatable food, but also bitterness. Move up and down the ladder of abstraction from the level of ideas to the level of specific evidence and back.

6. In human experience, motivation is a cracked mirror, never providing a pure reflection. Avoid, in both fiction and nonfiction, any simple explanation for why characters make important choices.

7. Gather evidence until you reach a dominant feeling about your source. Present that evidence—without editorial opinion—to influence (but not determine) the reader's response. Show and tell when you must, with a preference for showing.

9

X

X-raying *Miss Lonelyhearts* and *A Visit from the Goon Squad*

Texts Within Texts

Writers and readers love texts within texts. This writing strategy is as old as storytelling itself. Book 8 of the *Odyssey* contains several stories from the blind poet Demódokus about the Trojan War and the jealousy of the Greek gods, all told within the larger narrative of the great journey of Odysseus back to his homeland. In this chapter we will examine a number of works, fiction and nonfiction, that depend upon embedded text to solve narrative problems and advance a story. Prominent will be two great American novels written almost eighty years apart: *Miss Lonelyhearts*, by Nathanael West, who builds his story from letters to an advice columnist, and *A Visit from the Goon Squad,* by Jennifer Egan, who turns a PowerPoint presentation into a moving seventy-five-page chapter.

LETTERS FROM THE HEART

Some forms of narrative make more explicit use of embedded text than others, a case in point being the Depression-era novel *Miss Lonelyhearts.* A popular short novel into the 1970s, it has lost some of its dark charm with the passage of time, but it is an American classic that deserves rediscovery and X-ray reading.

In an introduction to the 2009 edition, novelist Jonathan Lethem appreciates this explanatory passage spoken by the narrator, which Lethem describes as "so disconcertingly clean and direct that it could remind you of a Hollywood 'treatment,'" that is, a pitch for creating a movie:

> Perhaps I can make you understand. Let's start from the beginning. A man is hired to give advice to the readers of a newspaper. The job is a circulation stunt and the whole staff considers it a joke. He welcomes the job, for it might lead to a gossip column, and anyway he's tired of being a leg man. He too considers the job a joke, but after several months at it, the joke begins to escape him. He sees that the majority of the letters are profoundly humble pleas for moral and spiritual advice, that they are inarticulate expressions of genuine suffering. He also discovers that his correspondents take him seriously. For the first time in his life, he is forced to examine the values by which he

lives. This examination shows him that he is the victim of the joke and not its perpetrator.

Not surprisingly, according to Lethem, "*Lonelyhearts* was inspired by access West was given to real letters written to a real advice columnist."

One of the first texts within the text we encounter is scribbled by a newspaper editor named Shrike, who makes fun of the advice columnist with a parody of prayer written on a piece of white cardboard and posted in the newsroom:

> Soul of Miss L, glorify me.
> Body of Miss L, nourish me.
> Blood of Miss L, intoxicate me.
> Tears of Miss L, wash me.
> Oh good Miss L, excuse my plea,
> And hide me in your heart,
> And defend me from mine enemies.
> Help me, Miss L, help me, help me.
> In sæcula sæculorum. Amen.

The use of this fake litany establishes the unorthodox structure of the novel, which is magnified by a series of letters written by the hopeless. Here is the first in its entirety. The grammatical and spelling mistakes are intentional:

Dear Miss Lonelyhearts —

I am in such pain I dont know what to do sometimes I think I will kill myself my kidneys hurt so much. My husband thinks no woman can be a good catholic and not have children irregardless of the pain. I was married honorable from our church but I never knew what married life meant as I never was told about man and wife. My grandmother never told me and she was the only mother I had but made a big mistake by not telling me as it dont pay to be inocent and is only a big disapointment. I have 7 children in 12 yrs and ever since the last 2 I have been so sick. I was operatored on twice and my husband promised no more children on the doctors advice as he said I might die but when I got back from the hospital he broke his promise and now I am going to have a baby and I don't think I can stand it my kidneys hurt so much. I am so sick and scared because I cant have an abortion on account of being a catholic and my husband so religious. I cry all the time it hurts so much and I don't know what to do.

Yours respectfully
Sick-of-it-all

Immediately clear is that such letters are written in a different voice and different style from that of the novel's narrator. This is reflected most obviously in elements of language and diction, from the variations from Standard English and punctuation to the malapropism *operatored*. But such stylistic flourishes are secondary to the poignant, pathetic nature of the narrative. It's only about two hundred words in length, yet its story grips the reader—a snapshot of the suffering of women, the tyranny of men, and the consequences of ignorance and narrow-mindedness. The line that really gets me is "it dont pay to be inocent."

But the problems of life extend not just from injustice but also from fate, a truth revealed in the letter written by a sixteen-year-old girl who is "born without a nose."

> I sit and look at myself all day and cry. I have a big hole in the middle of my face that scares people even myself so I cant blame the boys for not wanting to take me out. My mother loves me, but she crys terrible when she looks at me.
>
> What did I do to deserve such a terrible bad fate? Even if I did do some bad things I didnt do any before I was a year old and I was born this way. I asked Papa and he says he doesnt know, but that maybe I did something in the other world before I was born or that maybe I was being punished for his sins. I dont believe that because he is a very nice man. Ought I commit suicide?
>
> Sincerely yours,
> Desperate

Notice how the style of letter and voice of writer differ between the teenage girl and the hopeless mother. The former shows less language maturity ("she crys terrible") and greater desperation. An accident of birth at a time when remediation in the form of surgery was impossible turns into a tragic and ultimately hopeless cry against the fates that control the course of human life.

From these examples we begin to see the endless range of

possibilities for placing texts inside of texts—let's take it to another level—inside of texts. Imagine a story in which a man finds an old newspaper in an attic. He opens it up and sees a photo of his father along with a story about his involvement in a crime. Inside the story, an attorney quotes the words of an alleged suicide note. In the margins next to this story is a tidy note written in a woman's hand, probably his mother's. It reads "Not guilty by reason of insanity!!!" Texts galore, all converging and diverging to form the elements of a dramatic story.

POINTS OF POWER

Jennifer Egan won a Pulitzer Prize for her inventive and adventurous novel *A Visit from the Goon Squad*. This sprawling tale of the music business follows about a dozen characters over the course of forty years, including into the digital future, and experiments with every postmodern trick in the book. The most prominent of these is chapter 12, a seventy-five-page tour de force supposedly written by a character named Alison Blake in the form of a PowerPoint presentation. Each page is designed to resemble a PowerPoint slide.

My favorite is entitled "Facts About Dad," which is designed as a series of file folders viewed from above. From left to right, they say:

- Right after he shaves, his skin will squeak if you push your finger across it.
- His hair is thick and wavy, unlike a lot of dads.

- He can still lift me onto his shoulders.
- When he chews I hear his teeth smash together. [Then in smaller type:] They should be in pieces, but they're strong and white.
- When he can't sleep, he walks into the desert.
- It's a mystery why he loves Mom so much.

Most remarkable is the way that Egan employs a different visual device on each slide to carry the embedded text. These include a pyramid, meshing gears, converging arrows, a flowchart, and many others.

Among the most creative is a seesaw in which a father is asking questions of his son, who is obsessed with music. To get the visual effect, imagine a heavy dad on one end of the seesaw and a light son on the other. The father's end is on the ground; the son's is in the air. Large dark circles contain the father's questions; small light circles contain the son's answers. In conventional typography it would look like this:

"How did the game go the other night?"

"We lost 5–2."

"How many at-bats did you have?"

"Three."

"Anything new at school today?"

"Nope."

"Did you have music class with Mom?"

"Not today."

"Any kids you feel like asking over to play?"

"I see them at school."

"Want to have a catch after dinner?"
"I'd rather play music."

Egan gives the son the final word, abandoning the circles for a cartoon speech balloon: "Can I play music, Dad?"

Such experiments in storytelling should be encouraging to writers of every generation. The basic strategy remains the same: one text embedded in another. But the type of text will change with the times and technology. For Homer it was poems from an oral tradition embedded in what comes down to us as a written epic. For West it was letters from the love-lorn, a popular newspaper form, part of a genre known cynically as the "sob story." For Egan, it is an often tiresome form of digital presentation, the PowerPoint, transformed into something it is rarely used for: a story of the human heart.

SIGNS OF THE TIMES

While text within text is a strategy that both West and Egan use transparently, other writers take more indirect paths, so that you hardly notice the technique. Texts, including sign-age, become an integral part of the scene, as does *Gatsby*'s famous billboard overlooking the valley of ashes:

> But above the gray land and the spasms of bleak dust which drift endlessly over it, you perceive, after a moment, the eyes of Doctor T. J. Eckleburg. The eyes of Doctor T. J. Eckleburg are blue and gigantic—their retinas are one yard high. They look out of no face, but, instead, from a pair of enormous yellow spectacles which pass over a

non-existent nose. Evidently some wild wag of an oculist set them there to fatten his practice in the borough of Queens, and then sank down himself into eternal blindness, or forgot them and moved away. But his eyes, dimmed a little by many paintless days under sun and rain, brood on over the solemn dumping ground.

This sign, planted early in the narrative, will assume symbolic proportions, even metaphysical ones, later as the mechanic Tom Wilson mourns the violent death of his wife. He explains to a neighbor what he said to his wife about her adultery:

> … "and I said 'God knows what you've been doing, everything you've been doing. You may fool me, but you can't fool God!'"
>
> Standing behind him, Michaelis saw with a shock that he was looking at the eyes of Doctor T. J. Eckleburg, which had just emerged, pale and enormous, from the dissolving night.
>
> "God sees everything," repeated Wilson.
>
> "That's an advertisement," Michaelis assured him.

In my X-ray reading of *Gatsby,* I've tried to identify as many additional examples of Fitzgerald making use of texts within texts as possible. Here's my list, with page numbers from my edition and effect on the story:

> p. 25. Sign on George Wilson's garage (introduces character)
> p. 29. Inventory of books and magazines on living room table (reveals social class and character)

p. 38. Narrator reads newspaper at train station (shows his state of mind)

p. 78. Lyrics from popular jazz song "The Sheik of Araby" (establishes popular cultural mood of the era, with sexual overtones)

. p. 95. Lyrics of "Ain't We Got Fun," including the telling line "The rich get richer and the poor get children" (social commentary)

p. 166. A letter of condolence from Meyer Wolfsheim (ties up loose ends)

p. 167. Reference to death notice in Chicago newspaper (news value)

p. 173. A copy of an old children's book called *Hopalong Cassidy,* a cowboy adventure, with Gatsby's childhood writing on the last flyleaf

This last use of the text within a text is particularly telling. The fact that it is a cowboy tale links the aspirations of the young Gatsby with the adventurous themes of the American West. More telling is the schedule of daily activities the young "Jimmy" wrote down, including his work, studies, and playtime. Below that is a list of "General Resolves":

No wasting time at Shafters or [a name, indecipherable]
No more smokeing or chewing.
Bath every other day
Read one improving book or magazine per week
Save $5.00 [crossed out] $3.00 per week
Be better to parents

This book, found by Gatsby's father, places the character of Gatsby thoroughly in the American grain, associating him with a host of self-improving American characters, beginning with Benjamin Franklin.

DIFFERENT GENRES

We've seen that a good story can feel like a hall of mirrors, a puzzle box, or a stack of Russian nesting dolls. The poem within a poem. The play within a play. The playhouse inside of a real house. It's Cuban bandleader Desi Arnaz playing Cuban bandleader Ricky Ricardo in *I Love Lucy*. It's *The Dick Van Dyke Show*, a comedy show about the making of a comedy show. I wrote my doctoral dissertation on *The Canterbury Tales*, a sequence of more than twenty stories told by pilgrims inside the frame story of a journey on horseback from London to Canterbury.

The creation of modern book-length fiction was helped along by a subgenre known as the epistolary novel. That strange word comes from the same root as *epistle*, or letter. In eighteenth-century novels such as *The Expedition of Humphry Clinker* by Tobias Smollett, narrative spins out from a series of letters sent and received by key characters.

I have encountered examples of nonfiction writing I could call "epistolary journalism." This occurs, I would argue, when a reporter advances a story by quoting extensively from the letters, journals, e-mail messages, instant messages, voice-mail messages, Facebook updates, tweets, and even yearbook autographs of key individuals. Such quotation has a strange power, serving as another form of monologue or dialogue.

In 2003 journalist Cathy Frye demonstrated how far such a strategy could be taken. In "Evil at the Door," an installment of an award-winning series entitled "Caught in the Web," Frye unfolds the story of a naive thirteen-year-old girl who is stalked online, kidnapped, and murdered. She tells much of the tale through e-mail exchanges between the girl and her killer:

Tazz2999: Hey Sweetie
modelbehavior63: hey
Tazz2999: how are you my angel?
modelbehavior63: ok...u
Tazz2999: better now that ur on sweetie

In 1996, when I wrote the narrative series "Three Little Words," about a family in which the father dies of AIDS, I was able to enter into the man's young life through the window of his high school yearbook, which contained many revealing autographs, and into his wife's life through a series of journals she kept during the years her children were born.

When you stumble upon these texts in the real world, they can be used as elements of existing stories, or they can act as the seeds for new ones. In January of 2014 my brothers and I found our mother's high school autograph book from 1934. She was the first person in her large extended immigrant family to graduate from high school—Washington Irving High School, in Manhattan. The book was filled with messages from her classmates and relatives, almost all of whom have passed away, including her brother Vincent, who died at the age of nineteen from tuberculosis just months before the discovery of antibiotics, which might have saved him. At the age of eleven, he wrote to his older sister Shirley in a boyish hand: "Whoever steals this book will grad-u-8 from Sing Sing." In the four corners of the page he wrote: "FOR...GET...ME...NOT." It was like a voice from the grave—the only words left behind by the uncle we never knew. It was surprisingly moving to discover and was the kind of text that might lend itself for inclusion in a book someday. Mission accomplished.

So by all means, let texts talk wherever they may appear. Use them to advance the narrative, signify character, reflect setting, establish mood and theme, and create a chorus of diverse, sometimes discordant voices, all to reveal the complexity of human life.

WRITING LESSONS

1. Use written communication between characters as a form of monologue or dialogue. In Jane Austen novels, this communication might have been in the form of an exchange of letters. In *Miss Lonelyhearts* messages are exchanged via a mass medium—the newspaper. In more contemporary works of fiction and nonfiction, such as *A Visit from the Goon Squad,* characters can speak to one another or to multiple audiences via an almost endless number of media platforms, from e-mail messages to Instagram to Twitter to PowerPoint.

2. Use every opportunity to choose texts as evidence in every possible form: public records, court documents,

obituaries, wedding announcements, epitaphs, graffiti, tat-
toos, baseball cards, fortune cookies, T-shirts, cereal boxes,
journals, diaries, letters, notes left in pockets—and, in the
digital age, blog posts, tweets, status updates, text messages,
and more.

3. When you introduce texts within your texts, you can
do so in three different ways:

- A single element, such as a purloined letter, embedded in a larger story can have special impact
because of its singularity—say, as a clue to solving
a mystery. The name Rosebud on a child's sled, for
example.
- Multiple similar elements—such as an exchange
of letters or text messages—can establish a predictable pattern that builds momentum and guides
readers toward a destination.
- Multiple diverse textual elements—like the ones
in *Gatsby*—can surprise the reader even as they
eventually combine to create a setting, shape character, offer a dominant feeling, or express a theme.

10

X

X-raying *King Lear* and *The Grapes of Wrath*

Tests of Character

I remember listening to an audiobook version of *The Pillars of the Earth,* an epic novel by Ken Follett set in twelfth-century England and France, a story about a community of cathedral builders who try to do God's work in the face of the worst kinds of cruelty and corruption. In spite of a satisfying ending to a book of more than a thousand pages, I remember now and again yelling at the author through the speakers on the dashboard of my car: "Why can't you let those poor people alone! Haven't they suffered enough?"

Characters in stories suffer. It's what they do. It's how they suffer that gives meaning to life and wisdom to the readers of narratives of all kinds. Jesus suffers in the Gospels. Jews and other victims suffer in stories about the Holocaust. Families from Oklahoma suffer through the Dust Bowl and Depression as they make their way to California in *The Grapes of Wrath*.

Many writers have testified to the relationship between plot and character in all kinds of narrative writing, often with a focus on the suffering of protagonists. Good advice, for example, comes from Kurt Vonnegut, in his introduction to *Bagombo Snuff Box:*

- Give the reader at least one character he or she can root for.
- Every character should want something, even if it is only a glass of water.
- Be a sadist. No matter how sweet and innocent your leading characters, make awful things happen to them—in order that the reader may see what they are made of.

Let's consider two protagonists of popular British literature—James Bond and Harry Potter—to see how they stack up against Vonnegut's rubric:

1. *Rooting interest:* Both Bond and Potter get high marks here. Both have terrible enemies who threaten not just them but all of civilization and humankind. Bond and Potter are not kings or princes, but they have qualities that make us hope they succeed.

2. *Want:* Harry is an orphan who wants a home, a family, the love of his lost parents, and, most of all, friends. Bond wants women, liquor, fast cars, and other luxuries. But more important, he has a need to fulfill his mission, a license to

kill evil spies and terrorists in the name of queen and country.

3. *Sadism:* Bond is kidnapped, beaten, and tortured in the most bizarre ways by the most brutal and vicious enemies. In *On Her Majesty's Secret Service,* his bride is murdered. Goldfinger threatens to cut him from groin to brain with a laser. Harry loses his parents at birth and is raised by horrible relatives. In seven long novels he suffers capture, violence, torture, and threats, only to learn that he may have to die in order to kill the evil Lord Voldemort.

NAKED IN A STORM

King Lear is a good work to X-ray because of the way in which it measures the author's "sadism" toward his main character. In the story, which has a fairy-tale quality to it, Lear is old and tired of ruling. He wants to divide his kingdom among his three daughters—a terrible idea, of course, because two of the three women are monsters, and the third, Cordelia, will be exiled.

Before long, Lear will be stripped of everything—his retainers, his influence, his daughters, and his dignity, an emptying out (the word for this is *kenosis*) that finds him almost naked on the moors in a horrific storm accompanied by two allies: his fool and a madman. Here's the relevant passage:

> Lear: Thou wert better in a grave than to answer with thy uncovered body this extremity of the skies.—Is man no more than this? Consider him well.—Thou ow'st the worm no silk, the beast no hide, the sheep no wool, the cat no perfume. Ha, here's three on 's are sophisticated. Thou

art the thing itself; unaccommodated man is no more but
such a poor, bare, forked animal as thou art. Off, off, you
lendings! Come, unbutton here. [Tearing off his clothes.]

Fool: Prithee, nuncle, be contented. 'Tis a naughty night
to swim in. Now, a little fire in a wild field were like an old
lecher's heart—a small spark, all the rest on 's body cold.

Even in a brilliant production of the play—like the one I wit-
nessed in Stratford, England—it is hard to hear this amazing
exchange between the king and his fool. The special effects creating the sound and light of the storm tend to stifle the language, making an X-ray reading of the text especially desirable.

In this tempest, a scene of frenzied loss and despair, Lear
waxes his most philosophical. Unlike Macbeth, he is not
nihilistic. Lear has committed no crime. Instead he becomes
a kind of demented anthropologist, measuring the thin
veneer of civilization. He and his ragtag retainers are stripped
of the courtly trappings provided by creatures such as the
silkworm. Without these, man is a "poor, bare, forked animal," as humbling a phrase as has ever been directed at
humankind. Action echoes thought as he strips himself of
his "lendings," the coverings lent to him.

Macbeth had no fool to spark him back to sanity. So it is
wonderful that Lear's pathetic ranting is followed by a clever,
bawdy joke about the sexual incapacities of old lechers. They
may feel that certain spark, but it's not enough to heat them
up. It's exactly the mixture of tragic and comic that makes
Shakespeare unequaled as a playwright.

It is important to note that this moment of naked vul-
nerability and despair occurs in the structural middle of the

play: act 3, scene 4. At the beginning of the play, Lear is the most powerful man in the kingdom. By the middle, he is a naked animal howling at the heavens. During the remainder of the play, through the help of loyal friends and followers and his loving daughter Cordelia, Lear will be slowly restored to some semblance of dignified humanity. In the end, Cordelia will die and Lear will die, and from such suffering a tragic sense of the human self will be restored.

LIFELINES FROM DESPAIR

The suffering of Lear was so profound that some audiences and critics found it intolerable, resulting in at least one rewrite of the play with a happy ending. One wonders what that hack might have done with a revision of *The Grapes of Wrath*. Turn the Joad family into rich vintners in the Napa Valley?

The Joads go through hell. There is no midpoint of the narrative where all seems lost, followed by a movement toward restoration or reconciliation. For the Joads, there is only loss, loss, loss. The reader feels it on page after page. "I've done my damndest," wrote Steinbeck, "to rip a reader's nerves to rags." Point taken, but it never feels as if the *author* is the sadist. The sadists are those evildoers in the story: "I want to put a tag of shame," he wrote, "on the greedy bastards who are responsible for this [the Depression and its effects]." Those greedy bastards—corrupt business owners, crooked cops, and dishonest politicians—populate the novel. Their counterparts in the real world criticized the novel as "communist propaganda." Capitalists saw real threats in Steinbeck's advocacy for the working poor, whether he was championing government reforms or the strengthening of labor unions.

To return to Vonnegut's rubric, the Joad family fits all three criteria: they attract our sympathy, they want desperately to climb out of poverty, and they suffer time and again, until we realize late into the novel that every decision they have made, every action they have taken, is futile. The reader's nerves are like rags, as the author intended. But this does not mean there is not a lifeline, however thin, for us to grasp. Two of them, in fact.

The first comes when Tom Joad explains to Ma that he has had a vision of how poor farmers might come together in a communal effort to improve their plight. Be their own police; grow their own economy. Ma worries that her son will be killed by the cops, that she will never learn what happens to him. He responds that "a fella ain't got a soul of his own, but on'y a piece of a big one—an'then—"

"Then what, Tom?"

"Then it don' matter. Then I'll be all aroun' in the dark. I'll be ever'where—wherever you look. Wherever they's a fight so hungry people can eat, I'll be there. Wherever they's a cop beatin' up a guy, I'll be there. . . . I'll be in the way guys yell when they're mad an'—I'll be in the way kids laugh when they're hungry an' they know supper's ready. An' when our folks eat the stuff they raise an' live in the houses they build—why, I'll be there. See?"

This text has acquired the force of a credo or an anthem, the kind of working-class moral vision that inspired the likes of Bruce

Springsteen to write songs in honor of Tom Joad. If we X-ray the passage, the first thing we notice is that it is delivered as part of a dialogue with Ma, in what feels like the authentic dialect of a Dust Bowl–era Oklahoma farmer. It manages to merge the interests of the individual with that of the collective. While most of this is expressed in the plural (hungry people, kids, our folks), there is also the particular, as when "a cop" is beating up "a guy."

MYSTERY AT THE END

The novel is almost finished at this point, but it is not Tom who has the last word. It is Ma and her pregnant daughter, Rose of Sharon, our second lifeline. Her husband has run off, and probably because of malnutrition and the harsh conditions of the boxcar camps, Rose delivers a stillborn child. More death, emptiness, and futility.

During a torrential storm, like the one in *King Lear,* the Joads seek shelter in a barn and stumble upon a starving father and his son. The son explains that the father gave him what little food they had and had not eaten for six days. The son shares an old blanket with Ma, who covers Rose of Sharon with it. Rose of Sharon is hungry, soaked, and suffering from the effects of the stillborn delivery. Ma helps her daughter out of her wet clothes and wraps her in the blanket. Ma tries to care for the son. Then it happens:

> Suddenly the boy cried, "He's dyin', I tell you! He's starvin' to death, I tell you."
>
> "Hush," said Ma. She looked at Pa and Uncle John standing helplessly gazing at the sick man. She looked at

Rose of Sharon huddled in the comfort. Ma's eyes passed Rose of Sharon's eyes, and then came back to them. And the two women looked deep into each other. The girl's breath came short and gasping.

She said "Yes."

Ma smiled. "I knowed you would. I knowed!"

Ma then escorts the onlookers out of the barn into a tool-shed, "and she closed the squeaking door."

For a minute Rose of Sharon sat still in the whispering barn. Then she hoisted her tired body up and drew the comfort about her. She moved slowly to the corner and stood looking down at the wasted face, into the wide, frightened eyes. Then slowly she lay down beside him. He shook his head slowly from side to side. Rose of Sharon loosed one side of the blanket and bared her breast. "You got to," she said. She squirmed closer and pulled his head close. "There!" she said. "There." Her hand moved behind his head and supported it. Her fingers moved gently in his hair. She looked up and across the barn, and her lips came together and smiled mysteriously.

I daresay this ending rivals *Gatsby*'s as one of the greatest in American literature. The key difference is that Gatsby ends with a narrator's reflection. *The Grapes of Wrath* ends with a character's actions. It may be one of the only great endings whose final word is an adverb. Like the Mona Lisa, Rose of Sharon smiles mysteriously. As I focus my X-ray glasses on that word, I see it working on two levels, at least. The first comes from the context of the action. Why would a girl be smiling when she has suffered so much, when she is in the middle of an act that most human beings would find appalling and physically repulsive? One answer is that—in the midst of so much futility—this selfless act is giving nourishment to a starving man. But on a second level, *mysteriously* has the word *mystery* inside it. And that word has a religious connotation. Rose of Sharon (a common appellation for the Virgin Mary) is the starving Madonna, whose child is a grizzled, starving old man.

We've covered a lot of ground in this chapter, from Elizabethan England to Dust Bowl America, with glances forward to James Bond and Harry Potter. Let's conclude by looking back to Aristotle, who lived and worked three centuries before the Christian era. Aristotle thought and wrote on an endless number of topics, from practical science to ethics. For writers, his most useful theories are literary, especially those involving the experience of tragedy. What happens to a person who walks into an amphitheater to vicariously experience, say, the blinding of Oedipus Rex? (Or the degradation of King Lear?) What do we experience when we are reading or viewing the play? Aristotle called it catharsis, a word that endures in the English language. He defined it as "the purging of emotions of pity and fear."

Pity is what we experience when we identify with another human being to feel his or her pain. It draws us closer to the fallen protagonist. But we also feel fear. We are afraid that the forces that control the universe could descend upon us and doom us to the same fate of suffering and death. It is fear that drives us away from the protagonist, directing us out of the theater with the knowledge that the previous two hours were an illusion.

WRITING LESSONS

1. It is often the friction between opposites that generates the most dazzling effects. No friction, no heat. No heat, no light. No light, no wisdom. In Shakespeare, wisdom often comes from the lips of fools, as it does when Lear's fool tames his master's dark vision of mankind with a bawdy joke. Don't be afraid to mix the comic and the tragic.

2. As you imagine the arc of a story, think of the middle as a place where all seems lost, but also as a place from which important characters and values can be restored. The middles of stories, both fiction and nonfiction, never get the attention they deserve, elbowed out of the picture by their more beautiful siblings: beginnings and endings.

3. I've harped on the power of a single word at the end of a passage. It's powerful at the end of a sentence, but more and more powerful as the text grows to paragraph, passage, chapter, and the work itself. I've always thought of adverbs as weak parts of speech until I noticed that Steinbeck ended his greatest work with the word *mysteriously.*

4. Always remember that your stories are forms of vicarious experience. You have the ability to influence, though not control, your readers' attachment to characters. You can shape those characters so that we identify with their struggles. And you can make them suffer so that, in Vonnegut's good words, we can see what they are made of.

11

X

X-raying Gabriel García Márquez

Making It Strange

One morning in April of 2014, on the front page of the *Tampa Bay Times*, I read the news that Gabriel García Márquez had died at the age of eighty-seven. He was a towering literary figure of the last century—journalist, novelist, essayist, public intellectual, and Nobel laureate. His fiction became a pillar in a literary movement known as magical realism, an oxymoron that elevated the work of a school of South American authors and gained it global attention.

A journalist at heart who wrote for newspapers in Colombia during the 1950s, García Márquez expressed dissatisfaction with the "magical" part of that literary equation, arguing that every word he had ever written was grounded in experience.

Colette Bancroft, book editor of the *Tampa Bay Times*,

included in her tribute to García Márquez the author's most famous passage, the first sentence of his novel *One Hundred Years of Solitude:*

> Many years later, as he faced the firing squad, Colonel Aureliano Buendía was to remember that distant afternoon when his father took him to discover ice. At that time Macondo was a village of twenty adobe houses, built on the bank of a river of clear water that ran along a bed of polished stones, which were white and enormous, like prehistoric eggs. The world was so recent that many things lacked names, and in order to indicate them it was necessary to point.

The original, of course, was written in Spanish, *Cien años de soledad,* and subsequently translated by Gregory Rabassa.

PORTALS INTO STORIES

Those three celebrated sentences sit atop fifteen others to constitute the first paragraph of García Márquez's most famous book. In journalistic terms, eighteen sentences would add up to an impossible lead, an impenetrable block of text, bulkier than some complete stories that appear in a newspaper or on a website. For a four-hundred-page novel that covers the history of several generations of Colombian myth and magic, a sprawling first paragraph feels right, an invitation to dive into a swift river or to jump on board a moving train, a way of transporting ourselves from wherever we sit into a richly imagined fictional world.

But let's return to those first three sentences. Let's don our X-ray glasses and look beneath the surface of the text to see what's bubbling down below. If we can figure out what makes this famous passage so famous, perhaps we can add some sophisticated tools to our own writing workbenches.

Many years later... An odd way to begin a novel, but it generates a question: Later than what? It reminds us that the most powerful form of transportation in a narrative is the river of time. Time flows. Stories flow. But authors have the ability to violate natural laws of time, to make the past present and to invent the future.

As he faced the firing squad... It is not unusual for a journalist to plant a detail in a lead that will bear fruit later in the work. This adverbial reference to a dramatic event in the future of the narrative reveals much about the kind of story we are about to experience, one in which there is danger, intrigue, and military styles of capital punishment.

Colonel Aureliano Buendía was to remember that distant afternoon... The subject of the sentence is a character with a military title. The name Aureliano will be particularly important, as it will survive across generations as the name of children and grandchildren who will inherit or reject the legacy of their ancestors. The verb form "was to remember" has a conditional quality to it. Memory is persistent, as Salvador Dalí reminds us with his surrealistic images of melting watches, but it comes and goes. And it generates its own flawed narrative of the past at the most surprising moments, even when one is facing the firing squad.

CIRCLES AND LINES OF TIME

When his father took him to discover ice... The memory leads Aureliano back to his father as time seems to move in all directions. This first sentence ends—as most great sentences do—with an emphatic element, the discovery of ice (*el hielo*). That detail denotes something in the distant past, a subtropical setting in which ice is not ubiquitous but odd and mysterious. In a move journalists will recognize, this mention of ice in the lead sentence is fully realized at the end of the first chapter, when father and son pay money at a gypsy carnival to see and put their hands on this alchemical element.

At that time Macondo was a village of twenty adobe houses... Writers of narrative build little worlds that are inhabited by characters. They are worlds readers can visit, and the more we can "see" these microcosms, the richer will be our vicarious experience. The author transports readers back in time and to another place.

Built on the bank of a river of clear water... The river is a powerful archetype of time and change. But it exists only within the controlling boundaries of the banks. Without banks, the river becomes a flood, a destructive sea. Historian Will Durant used that metaphor to describe the distinction between history and civilization: "Civilization is a stream with banks. The stream is sometimes filled with blood from people killing, stealing, shouting and doing things historians usually record, while on the banks, unnoticed, people build homes, make love, raise children, sing songs, write poetry and even whittle statues. The story of civilization is the story of what happened on the banks. Historians are pessimists because they ignore the banks for the river." García Márquez understands the power of both the banks and the river.

That ran along a bed of polished stones, which were white and enormous, like prehistoric eggs... The author gives us more to see as we gaze down through the clear water, but it is the simile that seals the deal. The stones are like prehistoric eggs, once organic, life-containing objects now petrified by time and the forces of nature. Yet in this magical place, one imagines they could crack open in an instant, generating an army of dinosaurs or flying fish.

The world was so recent that many things lacked names... More manipulation of time here, but also an allusion that seems biblical. This feels like Genesis — the beginning, when God gave mankind dominion over the world by investing human beings with the power of naming. No human being has greater power to name than does the poet.

And in order to indicate them it was necessary to point... The author reminds us that language, however inherent in the human experience, is learned. The act of pointing has many purposes: to recognize, share, warn, call attention to, desire. I want that. Over there. Even babies do it.

MAKING THE FAMILIAR STRANGE

There is an awkward literary term that defines García Márquez's technique. It's called defamiliarization. It sounds better in a phrase: "to make the familiar strange." Journalists are more likely to flip it—to make the strange familiar—but there will be those times when we ask readers to see something they think they know in a completely new way.

Let's return to the discovery of ice.

Imagine that you are experiencing ice for the first time. (There are many Floridians, it occurs to me, who have never experienced snow. But ice is as close as the nearest margarita.) This is where the genius of García Márquez becomes palpable:

> When it was opened by the giant, the chest gave off a glacial exhalation. Inside there was only an enormous, transparent block with infinite internal needles in which the light of the sunset was broken up into colored stars....
>
> "It's the largest diamond in the world."
>
> "No," the gypsy countered. "It's ice."
>
> ...Little José Arcadio refused to touch it. Aureliano, on the other hand, took a step forward and put his hand on it, withdrawing it immediately. "It's boiling," he exclaimed, startled....
>
> [Their father] paid another five reales and with his hand on the cake [of ice], as if giving testimony on the holy scriptures, he exclaimed:
>
> "This is the great invention of our time."

I might argue that the great invention of our time—of all time—is the human brain. Its evolution gave us language, which gave birth to our ability to tell stories. Those stories can describe things that really happened, as in García Márquez's 1955 work, *The Story of a Shipwrecked Sailor*. More miraculously, they can contain things that never happened, that are imagined, a gift of God or nature that enriches our experience a thousandfold.

WRITING LESSONS

1. Think of a writing strategy as a form of ophthalmology. You are working on sharpening the vision of the reader. In Joseph Conrad's phrase, you will make the reader "see."

2. For narrative and investigative purposes, develop a time line. Plot events or scenes in chronological order, then examine opportunities for time inversions.

3. In a civic sense, your job as a writer is to make the strange familiar—to uproot corruption, translate jargon, show us how it works. In a literary sense, look for ways to make the familiar strange. What does the bottom of your shoe look like? What does it look like to a shoe salesman or a lover? What does it look like to a fire ant?

4. Try García Márquez's trick: imagine you are seeing a familiar thing for the first time, not knowing its function. For García Márquez it was a block of ice. How might you describe a hat, a cell phone, a banana, a cactus plant, your left ear?

12

X

X-raying Homer, Virgil, Roth — and Hitchcock

Zooming In

It was author David Finkel who taught me to "report cinematically." This was key, he argued, to writing a story that feels like a movie, using the variety of camera angles available to the cinematographer, from wide establishing shots to extreme close-ups. Creating such a story, writing coach Donald Murray advised, requires the author to "alter the distance between the writer and the subject matter." Out in the field, this means standing on a hilltop to observe and describe the battlefield below, then getting close enough to read the tattoo on the back of a soldier's hand. These days, such images can be captured in still shots and videos via the cell phone. For the dutiful writer, a notebook is the best kind of camera.

Where did the creators of cinema learn to write cinematically? There were precedents in the history of the visual arts, from cave paintings to tapestries to landscape paintings to portraits to photographs. Some of these showed scenes from a distance, others from close up. But where did those visual artists learn the master tricks of distance, perspective, and point of view?

POINT OF VIEW

I am about to make the case that it was the oral poet, then the writer of texts, who invented and perfected forms of visual composition. Homer surely had his moments. He could render an establishing crowd shot:

> And soon the assembly ground and seats were filled
> with curious men, a throng who peered and saw
> the master mind of war, Laertes' son.

And he could do the close-up, as when, upon his return home after a twenty-year absence, Odysseus is revealed to his old nurse by a scar from a wound inflicted long ago by "a wild boar's flashing tusk." The moment is vivid and appealing to the senses:

> This was the scar the old nurse recognized;
> she traced it under her spread hands, then let go,
> and into the basin fell the lower leg
> making the bronze clang, sloshing the water out.

Sometimes a visual image is projected directly from narrator to audience, but at a more sophisticated level, it can come through the eyes of a character or characters. One name for this effect is "point of view." Suddenly we are seeing what a character sees and feels—the scar of the returning hero through the eyes and under the hands of his aged nurse.

One of the most interesting and chilling examples of pre-cinematic visual writing comes from the Roman poet Virgil, author of the epic *Aeneid*. In a 2006 translation by Robert Fagles, the poet describes a powerful storm at sea brought on by the goddess Juno against warriors trying to escape the aftermath of the Trojan War:

> Flinging cries
> as a screaming gust of the Northwind pounds against his sail,
> raising waves sky-high. The oars shatter, prow twists round,
> taking the breakers broadside on and over Aeneas' decks
> a mountain of water towers, massive, steep.
> Some men hang on billowing crests, some as the sea
> gapes, glimpse through the waves the bottom waiting,
> a surge aswirl with sand.

Let's understand what we are seeing here. Through the narrator's description we see wind pounding on the sail, with waves rising above the height of the ship, then crashing down upon it, shattering the oars and twisting the ship around. The waves ascend to the height of a mountain, with some men swept overboard, clinging to the crests, and staring down. Into what? Into the sandy bottom of the sea. The place that awaits them: their sandy, watery grave. Two millennia before anyone dreamed of an aerial shot or the special effects used in the movies *Titanic* or *The Perfect Storm,* there was old Virgil creating—in language—the vertiginous seascape of the drowning sailors.

About two thousand years before atomic war unleashed Godzilla over Japan, a war in Troy, chronicled by Virgil, gave us this scene:

> I cringe to recall it now—look there!
> Over the calm deep straits off Tenedos swim
> twin, giant serpents, rearing in coils, breasting
> the sea-swell side by side, plunging toward the shore,
> their heads, their blood-red crests surging over the waves,
> their bodies thrashing, backs rolling in coil on mammoth coil
> and the wake behind them churns in a roar of foaming spray,
> and now, their eyes glittering, shot with blood and fire,
> flickering tongues licking their hissing maws, yes, now
> they're about to land. We blanch at the sight, we scatter.

I love how this passage begins and ends with a short sentence. In between is one amazing sentence, coiling and uncoiling like the serpents it describes, directing our eyes back and forth, in and out, from the action of the serpents to the movement of the sea, then close enough to see eyes of blood and fire.

ZOOMING IN AND OUT

The cinematic idea of seeing things from a distance and then zooming in continues to be a favorite move of creative filmmakers. In one recent film, *Gravity,* the effect is as dramatic as I've ever seen it, enhanced, of course, by 3-D glasses. The movie concerns two astronauts marooned in space, and the vantage point ranges from the star-spangled infinity of outer space to the fog of breath clouding the visor of a space suit. At one moment, you are peering into the blackness of space; at the next, a single loose bolt comes floating toward your hand.

Famously, Alfred Hitchcock showed us how this could be done in a single continuous shot. In the 1946 movie *Notorious,* starring Cary Grant and Ingrid Bergman, the leading lady is seen at a festive party in a huge mansion from the vantage point of someone at the very top of a tall spiral staircase. Bergman's character seems relaxed and social. Chatting with her is Claude Rains, a former Nazi operative, greeting guests, until the camera pans through the air, getting closer and closer, until it moves to the left of her figure and down to her left hand, which is curled shut. Then she opens it slightly, and the tightest close-up reveals for a second that she is holding a key. The whole scene takes about forty seconds.

Author Philip Roth grew up watching movies, and you can see their influence in the perspective of key characters in his fiction. The story "The Conversion of the Jews," for example, ends with a startling visual effect. The main character, a young Jewish boy named Ozzie, escapes from a harsh religious-school experience by climbing to the top of a synagogue and threatening to jump off. Mother and rabbi plead that he come down to safety even as a group of firemen holds open a safety net.

> "Promise me, promise me you'll never hit anybody about God."

He had asked only his mother, but for some reason everyone kneeling in the street promised he would never hit anybody about God.

Once again there was silence.

"I can come down now, Mamma," the boy on the roof finally said. He turned his head both ways as though checking the traffic lights. "Now I can come down…"

And he did, right into the center of the yellow net that glowed in the evening's edge like an overgrown halo.

Notice the quick shift of point of view, from the boy turning his head both ways, which could be seen by those below, to the glowing safety net, which can only be seen from the perspective of the jumping boy.

DETAILS OF CHARACTER AND STORY

While I've described these movements—from close-up to distance—as cinematic or literary, what makes them most powerful is that they are human. It is the way we see. As I sit at my computer, I see letters track across my screen as my hands move about the keyboard. I look up and to the right and see on the wall a political campaign poster from the 1930s featuring my grandfather Peter Marino. I look down at my left hand and see a tiny scar in the shape of a star sustained thirty years ago in a softball game. Now I look up and see a blast of light and blue sky through the skylight above my desk. A crisscross of oak beams supports the structure. My eyes return to the computer screen. Keyboard, poster, scar, skylight, keyboard.

Why turn your notebook into a camera? When it comes

to the marriage of craft and purpose, novelist Joseph Conrad said it best: "My task...is, by the power of the written word to make you hear, to make you feel—it is, before all, to make you *see*. That—and no more, and it is everything. If I succeed, you shall find there according to your deserts: encouragement, consolation, fear, charm—all you demand—and, perhaps, also that glimpse of truth for which you have forgotten to ask." Make me see.

WRITING LESSONS

1. Use your notebook as a camera. Capture events in a way they can unfold—as movie directors do. Now, smaller than your notebook is your mobile phone. You can use it to capture still photos or video and audio. These can be used in multimedia story forms, but they can also be an efficient way to find images that can be transformed into written text.

2. Learn the language of photo composition and cinematography, from establishing shot to close-up. Visuals imitate texts—and vice versa. Consider point of view. What does your character see, and what do you want your readers to see? An aerial view from the top of a staircase? A beautiful woman in a red gown? The key she is holding in her hand?

3. In your reporting or research or drafting, avoid the mistake of seeing the world from a predictable middle distance. Step back to take in the whole setting and context. Move close so you can see the pores of your character's skin. (I once interviewed the glamorous Farrah Fawcett up close during her glory days. She looked flawless until I saw her fiddling with her strappy sandal, revealing a blister on her heel.)

13

X

X-raying Chaucer

Pointing the Way

One of the first proverbs I learned as a child was "April showers bring May flowers." It was meant to suggest that good things can result from bad weather. Years later, the proverb grew an appendage: "What do May flowers bring?" The answer was "Pilgrims," punning on the name of the ship that landed at Plymouth Rock.

The poetic associations of springtime are as old as literature itself. At times because of snow and ice and the bareness of trees, the world seems dead. But then it returns to life. No writer expressed this symbolic pattern more artfully than Geoffrey Chaucer. That he set the standard in a single sentence earned him the title of the father of English poetry. Here is that sentence, written around 1380 in a dialect of what we now call Middle English. You will be able to recognize most of the words:

Whan that Aprill with his shoures soote
The droghte of March hath perced to the roote,
And bathed every veyne in swich licour
Of which vertu engendered is the flour;
Whan Zephirus eek with his sweet breeth
Inspired hath in every holt and heeth
The tendre croppes, and the yonge sonne
Hath in the Ram his halve cours yronne,
And smale foweles maken melodye,
That slepen al the nyght with open eye
(So priketh hem nature in hir corages);
Thanne longen folk to goon on pilgrimages,
And palmeres for to seken straunge strondes,
To ferne halwes, kowthe in sondry londes;
And specially from every shires ende
Of Engelond to Caunterbury they wende,
The hooly blisful martir for to seke,
That hem hath holpen whan that they were seeke.

Here it is again in my plain modern version:

When April with its sweet showers
The drought of March has pierced to the root
And bathed every vein with such liquid
By virtue then engendered is the flower;
When the West Wind with his sweet breath
Has inspired in every holt and heath
The tender crops, and the young sun
Has in the Ram his half course run,

And small birds make melody
That sleep all the night with open eyes
(As nature pricks them in their hearts),
Then folk long to go on pilgrimages
And palmers to seek unknown shores
To faraway shrines known in sundry lands;
And especially from every shire's end
Of England to Canterbury they wind,
The holy blissful martyr for to seek,
Who has helped them when they were sick.

THE DESTINATION SENTENCE

As someone who wrote a doctoral dissertation on Chaucer, I can attest that countless lessons of powerful writing flow from a study of his work. Here are just a few that can be observed from an X-ray reading of this single sentence:

• Weather is part of the setting of a story and can be used emblematically, even symbolically.

• The story of human lives can be reflected or echoed in manifestations of the natural order.

• Energy builds in a passage when the most significant element is reserved for the end.

The first eighteen lines of *The Canterbury Tales* can be described as a periodic sentence. This is the traditional name of a sentence that builds to a main clause near its end, near the period, hence the name periodic. This structure stands apart from the more common "loose" construction, in which the main action occurs at the beginning and all the lesser elements follow.

There is another, newer way of thinking about these structures. Think of a loose sentence as "branching to the right"; that is, the main clause appears at the beginning and all the subordinate elements branch to the right (as if the entire sentence appeared on a single line).

In Chaucer's case, the main clause would sit on the right, with all the earlier clauses branching to the left.

Your X-ray reading will help you identify the main clause as well as the branches in most sentences. This is an important distinction because the rhetorical effects of these two sentence structures are so different. One effect of the right-branching sentence is clarity, created when the subject and the verb of the main clause come early in the sentence. Meaning is established right away, and the writer can add an infinite number of supporting elements: "We go to grandmother's house, over the river and through the woods." Sentences like Chaucer's have a different effect. They build and build and build, leading to something interesting and/or important. Which is why the song lyric is "Over the river and through the woods to grandmother's house we go."

Before we get to the main point of Chaucer's story, the urge to go on pilgrimages, he requires us to take a journey through the effects of April's arrival on wintry England: from rains to plants to flowers; from the movement of the west wind to the progression of the heavenly spheres; from the musical energy of the birds to the rousing of the folk.

Whether sentences are loose or periodic, their length

alone sends a message. And while the average length of sentences in Standard English prose continues to shrink, the long sentence has many valuable uses, especially to create the effect of being taken on a journey, of flying over a landscape or cruising through a tunnel.

YOUR THEME IN A WORD

Here are more lessons to be drawn from Chaucer's first sentence and from the larger narrative pattern of his collection of tales:

- Time (natural and narrative) can be described as a cycle or a line — or both.
- Human character is revealed by the surface of things, but also by that which lies beneath the surface.
- Individual stories can be embedded in larger frames.
- Small stories and places can stand in for bigger ones.
- The broadest, deepest themes can often be expressed in a short phrase and at times in a single word.

We often conduct an exercise at the Poynter Institute, where I teach, in which we ask writers to choose one of their stories and describe its theme — or "what it's about" — in a single word. If Chaucer were in the workshop and I asked him that question, I imagine that his answer would be something like "rebirth" or, in a longer phrase, "coming back to life." Without reference to the Easter season, which often falls in April, Chaucer offers in a single sentence a brilliant catalog of regeneration. It's worth listing the key elements again:

- The rain invigorates the dormant roots.
- The life-giving liquid is absorbed through the plants, creating the flowers.
- The wind blows from the west, invigorating the woods and meadows.
- The sun moves through the constellation Aries, restarting the astrological cycle.
- The birds sing all night long in their procreative ecstasy.
- Human beings want to get outside and go, go, go.

There is an order here, as rejuvenation begins with elements such as rain and wind, which grow plants and flowers. The movement is from nonliving to living things, then to a higher order of living thing—the birds—and then from animal life to humanity.

This progression is constructed from two words, the first repeated: *when* and *then*.

When this happens,
When that happens,
Then this happens.

The "this" is that people of all kinds, liberated to some degree from the bad weather that keeps them huddled indoors, whether in huts or castles, venture out. Some of these folks travel all over the world to visit holy shrines. And from all over England, they head for Canterbury. Think, if you must, of spring break with a religious justification.

To use a distinction drawn by the theologian Saint Augustine of Hippo, the pilgrims seek their own revival from both sin and physical maladies by making the journey from the City of Man (London) to the City of God (Canterbury). Whether they are looking for absolution or a miraculous cure, there is hope that something that is dying—the body, the soul—can be brought back to life through the intercession of the holy blissful martyr Thomas Becket.

WEATHER AS CHARACTER AND METAPHOR

Think for a moment on the useful distinction—in both science and literature—between climate and weather. As we consider the implications of global warming, it is often hard to distinguish between short-term and long-term changes in metrics such as rainfall and temperature. Think of climate as broad and weather as narrow, or of climate as something that forms over time and weather as something that happens now. Earth's atmosphere may be heating up, even as Boston may be having a rough winter.

Chaucer seems to be talking about weather and climate at the same time—that is, in general, over long eras, nature and people behave a certain way in springtime. But this is the story of a particular group of pilgrims—including the character of Chaucer himself—who gather at the Tabard Inn.

Simply put, writers have to make decisions about the weather and how it will affect the action of a story. Think about it in these narrative patterns:

1. Weather can be used in harmony with character— what critics once called the pathetic fallacy. In other words,

the happy bride is married on a sunny day. The murder plot is hatched on a stormy night. The struggling, claustrophobic writer is snowbound (as in *The Shining*). In some cases, the weather causes the effects (the *Titanic* hits the iceberg). At times, it echoes an emotional message.

2. To avoid the pathetic fallacy and the cliché of a dark and stormy night, authors often choose a climate that exists in some tension with the plot. There is a famous passage in *The Red Badge of Courage* in which the young soldier, running from battle, stumbles into a clearing in the forest. The sun shines through the trees, creating the sense of a beautiful natural chapel, until the soldier stumbles upon the corpse of a dead soldier rotting on the ground.

3. There are times, as in *The Canterbury Tales*, when weather is used thematically: in this case, the spiritual rebirth of human beings is inspired by the natural regeneration of spring. T. S. Eliot, riffing on Chaucer, turns the tables, insisting in "The Waste Land" that April is actually the "cruellest month" because it breeds lilacs "out of the dead land."

Weather can also be used editorially, the best example coming from another of England's literary titans, Charles Dickens. This disquisition on London's fog serves as the introduction to *Bleak House*—and much more:

> Fog everywhere. Fog up the river, where it flows among green aits [islands] and meadows; fog down the river, where it rolls defiled among the tiers of shipping, and the waterside pollutions of a great (and dirty) city. Fog on the Essex marshes, fog on the Kentish heights. Fog creeping

into the cabooses of collier-brigs [coal transports]; fog lying out on the yards, and hovering in the rigging of great ships; fog drooping on the gunwales of barges and small boats. Fog in the eyes and throats of ancient Greenwich pensioners, wheezing by the firesides of their wards; fog in the stem and bowl of the afternoon pipe of the wrathful skipper, down in his close cabin; fog cruelly pinching the toes and fingers of his shivering little 'prentice boy on deck. Chance people on the bridges peeping over the parapets into a nether sky of fog, with fog all round them, as if they were up in a balloon, and hanging in the misty clouds.

I'm not sure I ever read a topic sentence for a paragraph as efficient as "Fog everywhere." It stands as a verbless sentence, as do all the other descriptive fragments in the passage. What follows "everywhere" is a catalog of specific places where the London fog works its depressive magic.

This catalog, like Chaucer's, has a logic worth noting. For Chaucer the movement of reawakening goes from rain to crops to wind to stars to birds to humans. Something parallel happens here, as the fog moves over rivers to landmasses to the instruments of human activity to modes of transportation and then into and across an interesting variety of human beings: from pensioner to ship captain to apprentice to sightseers on bridges. The other exemplification of "everywhere" is the movement of scale and perspective. "Everywhere" includes broad stretches of sky as well as spaces between the toes and fingers of the 'prentice boy on the deck of a ship. The captain experiences the fog in a claustrophobic cabin; those random folks looking over the side of the bridge have a kind of mystical displaced feeling of somehow standing in the sky.

Dickens is not yet finished with the fog in *Bleak House*. Before long it works its way into the legal system: "Never can there come fog too thick, never can there come mud and mire too deep, to assort with the groping and floundering condition which this High Court of Chancery, most pestilent of hoary sinners, holds, this day, in the sight of heaven and earth." *Bleak House* is generally recognized as one of Dickens's masterpieces, a startling collection of memorable characters connected in a serpentine plot of greed, longing, generosity, loss, and legacy. It also happens to be one of the sharpest critiques of a corrupt legal system in the history of literature. The instrument of justice turns out to be the harshest oppressor of humanity. That great fog provides the perfect setting for the work of pettifoggers, greedy and self-important lawyers who take advantage of the poor and the powerless. That thick fog makes justice blind but not impartial.

WRITING LESSONS

1. Most sentences you write are going to be loose, or right-branching, with the subject and verb of the main clause occurring early on. But there are special opportunities to take readers on a journey of understanding, as Chaucer does in his first sentence. A periodic sentence—think of it as a destination sentence—allows you to build and build to a

verb or main clause near the end, which can be used to sur-prise or reward the reader for following you on your journey.

2. Anytime you write a story or report, especially if you are stuck, try this strategy: think of what your work is about—what it is *really* about. Write down your theme. You can be as discursive as you want in a first draft, but as you proceed, exercise more discipline. Try writing your theme statement in five words or three or one. Chaucer might have written "rebirth." Dickens might have needed a few more: "The pervasive corruption of London's legal system." Once you know that theme, you can marshal the evidence you need to make it convincing.

3. When constructing a list, a catalog, or an inventory of revealing items, avoid the random. Look for an order: time, space, dimension, theme. In the beginnings of both *The Canterbury Tales* and *Bleak House* there is a logical order, a progression of elements that sets the thematic tone for an entire work.

4. Any long narrative will involve characters existing in a climate and moving through weather. In one sense it just pins down the effects of setting: the broiling sun of South Beach; the reliable rains of Seattle; the frigid grip of Ottawa in March. But the author has to make choices about which actions occur in what kinds of weather. A certain random purposefulness (sorry for the oxymoron) may offer writers the most choices and create the most realistic effects.

14

X

X-raying *Sir Gawain and the Green Knight*

Careless Wish

One of my favorite stories—a standard in the canon of English literature—is *Sir Gawain and the Green Knight.* The original version was written about 1400 by an unnamed poet writing in a northern dialect of Middle English, which—unlike Chaucer's dialect—is not accessible to the modern reader without a glossary. Fortunately, excellent translations exist. J. R. R. Tolkien, author of *The Lord of the Rings,* wrote one. A 2007 version by poet Simon Armitage captures the mood, style, and rhythm of the original. I will use it for my X-ray reading, referring to the original when necessary.

Here's the story in a nutshell. It is the holiday season in King Arthur's court, and a great celebration is under way, but Arthur is getting restless. This should be a magical time of the year, but he declares that he will not eat a bite until there is some holiday game set loose, some wonder to behold.

THE CARELESS WISH

Here we confront one of the oldest and most reliable story generators, the careless wish. It is the stuff of a hundred *I Dream of Jeannie* episodes: the owner of a magic lamp makes a wish only to see it lead in a bad direction or have unintended consequences. In mythology, we have the story of King Midas, who wants everything he touches to turn to gold—but as soon as his wish is granted, his beloved daughter turns to metal upon his touch. In nonfiction, we see the narrative wish played out as a condition of human aspiration. A wish to become an Olympic champion turns into an illegal effort with performance-enhancing drugs. The student gets into the school of her dreams but resorts to cheating when she can't achieve good grades. So back to King Arthur, who wants to see something truly magical. Be careful, Arthur, what you wish for.

Just as Arthur utters his wish, a giant of a knight appears at the door. He is on horseback and carries a huge ax, the blade measuring three feet from top to bottom. More astonishing, he is green from head to toe—and so is his horse. The king wanted a marvel, and now he has it. The Green Knight addresses the court and challenges Arthur's brave and illustrious knights to a Christmas game. He invites someone to grab his ax and chop off his green head. If the knight manages it, he gets to keep the great ax as a prize. If he fails, he must one year hence track down the Green Knight and offer his own head for a return blow. (Back in the day, in the schoolyard at Saint Aidan's, some of the big kids played a game in which they exchanged punches. The more confident kid gave his opponent "first shot." Who knew this went back at least to the Middle Ages?)

Of course, no knight accepts the challenge at first, which frustrates Arthur, who steps forward and grabs the ax. Embarrassed, a single humble knight, Sir Gawain, volunteers to stand in for his king. The poet will take it from here:

> In the standing position he [the Green Knight] prepared to
>   be struck,
> bent forward, revealing a flash of green flesh
> as he heaped his hair to the crown of his head,
> the nape of his neck now naked and ready.
> Gawain grips the axe and heaves it heavenwards,
> plants his left foot firmly on the floor in front,
> then swings it swiftly towards the bare skin.
> The cleanness of the strike cleaved the spinal cord
> and parted the fat and the flesh so far
> that the bright steel blade took a bite from the floor.
> The handsome head tumbles onto the earth
> And the king's men kick it as it clatters past.

The careless wish is the first cousin to the rash promise. *King Lear* begins with a rash promise — the king's statement that he will give the biggest share of his land to the daughter who proclaims to love him most. All hell breaks loose. Arthur wants his game, then he gets it. But both Arthur and

Gawain rashly and naively accept the terms of the beheading game. They should have known that this magical figure would have an escape hatch.

LOOK IT UP IN THE *OED*

To be a good X-ray reader, you must learn to overread, or overinterpret, a text. I am about to show you how it's done and why it's so much fun. The year of *Gawain*, remember, was around 1400, and we have left the Green Knight without his head. Recall the words of the poet:

> The handsome head tumbles onto the earth
> And the king's men kick it as it clatters past.

The question must be asked directly: In that final detail, as the courtiers kick around the severed head, are we looking at an allusion to English football, what Americans call soccer? Are the knights of the Round Table the progenitors of the champions of England's Premier League? This kind of speculation is a collateral benefit of X-ray reading. I don't know the answer yet, but I'm off to do a bit of research. I will follow the indispensable advice of my teacher Donald Fry: "Look it up in the *OED*, Roy." That is, the *Oxford English Dictionary*.

Okay, I'm back, and I have some good news. The earliest reference to the word *football*, according to the *OED*, occurs in 1424, in a Scottish king's prohibition of men playing "at the football." There are earlier references to the game in Latin, almost all of which remark on or take exception to the extreme violence associated with versions of the sport.

Here is an interesting note on the ancient analogues of the game from its international governing body's website, FIFA.com:

> Scholars have also suggested that besides the natural impulse to demonstrate strength and skill, in many cases pagan customs, especially fertility rites, provided a source of motivation for these early "footballers." The ball symbolized the sun, which had to be conquered in order to secure a bountiful harvest. The ball had to be propelled around, or across, a field so that the crops would flourish and the attacks of the opponents had to be warded off.

There may not be a more obvious fertility figure in English literature than the Green Knight and his green steed. And even if such speculation is way off base, there is something richly humorous in the idea of these elegant courtiers in the middle of their Christmas feast knocking around the severed head.

UP THE ANTE

The writer can bring too much attention to ghoulish detail, but in this case it's only to call attention to the squeamish discomfort of the courtiers. Now we are about to see another writing strategy in action — upping the ante:

> Blood gutters brightly against his green gown,
> yet the man doesn't shudder or stagger or sink
> but trudges towards them on those tree-trunk legs

and rummages around, reaches at their feet
and cops hold of his head and hoists it high,
and strides to his steed, snatches the bridle,
steps into the stirrup and swings into the saddle
still gripping his head by a handful of hair.
Then he settles himself in his seat with the ease
Of a man unmarked, never mind being minus his head!

Not amazing enough? The poet raises the ante some more. As the Green Knight holds up his head, the eyes open and it begins to speak, reminding Sir Gawain that he must pay his debt and receive the return blow one year thence at a mysterious place called the Green Chapel. With that he gallops off, head in hand, his hooves sparking fire in the flint.

And then?
Well, with the green man gone
they laughed and grinned again.
And yet such goings-on
were magic to those men.

Everyone is laughing and grinning—except, of course, Sir Gawain.

So far we are only five hundred lines into a twenty-five-hundred-line narrative poem. What follows is one wonderful passage after another: the dramatic and dreadful turning of the seasons as the fateful year passes; the girding of Sir Gawain on a great horse and with a marvelous shield; his dangerous passage through a fierce northern wasteland; his discovery of a castle and its peculiar lord; his attempted seduction by the lady of the castle; and his poetic comeuppance from the Green Knight—a mere nick on the neck for being a flawed but virtuous knight.

Once again we see that the incident that incites the narrative, to use a useful strategy from creative writing teacher Robert McKee, begins at a feast, a joyful ceremony that is part of a holiday festival. We should be convinced by now that one of our jobs as storytellers is to get most of the key players in the same place: a courtyard, a ballroom, a stadium, a church, a circus tent. Some characters will play key roles. Others will have bit parts. And some will be like extras in the movies, their only role being to kick the head away when it rolls toward their feet.

THE WASTELAND

Another part of the fun of X-ray reading is finding parallels between works as disparate as *Gawain* and *Gatsby*. The magical party is a connection we can draw between Gatsby and Gawain, as is the hero's dangerous dalliance with a married woman, as is the main character's passage through the symbolic geography of a dead landscape, a wasteland.

> Only diligence and faith in the face of death
> will keep him from becoming a corpse or carrion.
> And the wars were one thing, but winter was worse:
> clouds shed their cargo of crystallized rain
> which froze as it fell to the frost-glazed earth.
> With nerves frozen numb he napped in his armor,
> bivouacked in the blackness amongst bare rocks

where meltwater streamed from the snow-capped summits
and high overhead hung chandeliers of ice.

This is the dread territory that separates the luxuries of
Arthur's court and the Green Chapel.

It interests me to see a similar pattern in *The Great
Gatsby*. The author gives us the vitality of Manhattan and
the luxuries of Long Island—separated by the wasteland he
describes as the valley of ashes:

> About half way between West Egg and New York the
> motor road hastily joins the railroad and runs beside it
> for a quarter of a mile, so as to shrink away from a certain
> desolate area of land. This is a valley of ashes—a fantas-
> tic farm where ashes grow like wheat into ridges and hills
> and grotesque gardens; where ashes take the forms of
> houses and chimneys and rising smoke and, finally, with
> a transcendent effort, of men who move dimly and
> already crumbling through the powdery air. Occasion-
> ally a line of gray cars crawls along an invisible track,
> gives out a ghastly creak, and comes to rest, and immedi-
> ately the ash-gray men swarm up with leaden spades and
> stir up an impenetrable cloud, which screens their
> obscure operations from your sight.

This may be one of the best paragraphs in American literature. It describes a polluted setting—the detritus of
wealth-generating industrialization—that becomes a kind
of poison swamp for all the characters who work or live
there and especially for those who must pass through it. If

the skyscrapers of the city and the mansions of the island become oases of escape, it is here in the valley where real life is played out, with all its despair, treachery, and violence. One of the collateral benefits of X-ray reading is the ability to recognize similar narrative patterns, even in work written centuries apart.

WRITING LESSONS

1. The careless wish and the rash promise are two ancient story motifs commonly associated with folk literature. But all such narrative archetypes have potential for use in contemporary stories, whether fiction or nonfiction. It is a universal condition to wish for something, a desire that too often produces a bad result. Don't be afraid to shape the stuff of experience with these older motifs as long as they don't exaggerate or distort your story.

2. How sharp was the Green Knight's ax? Sharpness is as sharpness does. Before you are tempted to describe a quality with a bland adjective, try showing the audience the evidence. Let them decide how sharp it is through the action of the blade.

3. Follow the severed head. It's a grisly detail, to be sure, but not every author would have bothered to follow the head after it had been severed from the body. It's another example of a pre-cinema cinematic detail—the "camera" following the rolling head and seeing it kicked along by the courtiers.

4. There may be no more pleasurable activity for a reader of old literature than to look up odd and interesting words and phrases in the *Oxford English Dictionary*. My

quest was to find the beginnings of English football, and the *OED* provided me not just with the origin of the word and a date but also with its link to violence.

5. What is so cool about *Gawain* is the way the author ups the ante — that is, raises the stakes of the narrative. This can be done any number of times in a story when you think the hero may have a problem and suddenly you realize that he has a *problem*. A boring Christmas feast is changed by the interruption of a spectacular creature whose appearance would be miraculous enough but whose actions raise again and again the stakes of the game.

6. Cross the wasteland. A virtue of X-ray reading is to recognize motifs in the work of writers centuries and cultures apart. For Gatsby, it means crossing the ever-dangerous valley of ashes to visit the castles of the Jazz Age. For Sir Gawain, a deadly wasteland must be crossed as a rite of passage before he can find the desired landscape. For writers, such forbidden areas can be natural — a stretch of desert — or man-made, such as a cemetery for junked cars.

15

X

X-raying *Macbeth*

Ends of Things

Although we do not know the exact day William Shakespeare was born, we celebrate his birthday on April 23. As of this writing, the Bard is four hundred and fifty years old. Because many of us will not be residents of this distracted globe when Will's big five-zero-zero comes around, we should do our best to praise him now and as often as we can for as long as we can. There is no one like him.

Those of you who have read my books or attended my classes know that I have a favorite Shakespeare sentence. It comes from *Macbeth* — or, as superstitious thespians refer to it, the Scottish play. Lady Macbeth dies offstage. When last we had seen her, she was crazed, washing the blood from her hands over and over, even when there wasn't a "damned spot" left. Later, one of Macbeth's attendants approaches him with the news: "The Queen, my lord, is dead."

Before I explain how this sentence forever changed my writing and teaching, a bit of backstory is in order. Several years ago, my daughter Alison Hastings performed in the Georgia Shakespeare production of *Macbeth* on Halloween weekend. Alison played one of the three witches, named the Weïrd Sisters by Shakespeare. In Shakespeare's time, *weird* had a different meaning from the modern sense of "super-crazy" and "unusual." Back then it meant "fated" or "destined," and it will be the prophecies of the Weïrd Sisters that help seal Macbeth's fate.

Macbeth is one of Shakespeare's shortest and bloodiest plays. When the Macbeths slaughter the king in their own castle, they have committed three of the gravest sins as understood within the Elizabethan and Jacobean moral order: they kill a king (regicide), they kill a kinsman (patricide), and they violate the covenants of hospitality — hosts are responsible for their guests' safety while they reside within the hosts' walls. At the end, Macbeth gets what he deserves. He is killed in battle offstage, an opportunity for one final shock, as his conqueror walks onto the stage with Macbeth's bloody head in his hand.

This is perfect Halloween stuff, and it was a joy to see Alison cavorting with her two very weird Weïrd Sisters, one played by a beefy gentleman. We watched two performances, and I then returned home to reread the play. Somehow I got hooked on the sentence "The Queen, my lord, is dead."

EMPHATIC WORD ORDER

My obsession with this sentence grew from the realization that Shakespeare did not have to write the sentence that way. He had at least two, if not three, other choices:

- The Queen is dead, my lord.
- My lord, the Queen is dead.
- And if the messenger had been Yoda of *Star Wars* fame, Macbeth may have had to deal with: "Dead the Queen is, my lord."

As you examine those three alternatives, recognize that there is nothing "wrong" with them. All four versions stand up to the scrutiny of Standard English, even though Yoda's version seems awkward and eccentric. In all four sentences, the six words are the same. But in each, the words roll out in a different order.

To honor Shakespeare, I profess that his version is the best — the best words in the best order. But such preferences cannot be just declared, they must be argued. Here, then, I make my case through an X-ray reading of "The Queen, my lord, is dead."

- A momentous announcement, the death of a queen, is made public in six quick words.
- Each word is one syllable long.
- The sentence has a clear beginning, middle, and ending — praise be to commas!

- The subject of the sentence — "The Queen" — appears immediately. Any sentence with such a beginning carries weight.
- The least significant element in the sentence, "my lord," appears in the middle, the position of least emphasis.
- The slight delay between subject and verb holds a nanosecond of suspense.
- The most important phrase, "is dead," appears at the end, the point of greatest emphasis.

This rhetorical strategy — placing the most emphatic word in a sentence at the end — is more than two thousand years old, but it felt new to me until Shakespeare's words slapped me good and hard. It has become for me weightier than a strategy, more like a theory of reading and writing — the fact that any phrase that appears near the end of a sentence or a paragraph or a chapter will receive special attention. What we call a period the Brits call a full stop — a better name, a rhetorical name, because it focuses our attention on the effects of an ended sentence. All humor and most oratory is marked by the repetition of this single strategy. Got something good, kid? Put it at the end.

THE ENDING AS HOT SPOT

It must be said that Macbeth's response to the news turns out to be much more famous than the message. "She should have died hereafter," he says. "There would have been a time for such a word." There's some ambiguity here. Some scholars think he means that she would have died eventually, in the natural order of things. But then this:

> Tomorrow and tomorrow and tomorrow
> Creeps in this petty pace from day to day
> To the last syllable of recorded time,
> And all our yesterdays have lighted fools
> The way to dusty death. Out, out, brief candle!
> Life's but a walking shadow, a poor player
> That struts and frets his hour upon the stage
> And then is heard no more. It is a tale
> Told by an idiot, full of sound and fury,
> Signifying nothing.

The poet has one big advantage over the prose writer. Writers of prose can emphasize a word by placing it at the end of a sentence. The poet doubles down by placing a key word at the end of a line. These words end sentences: *dusty death, brief candle, heard no more, signifying nothing.* Now add the energy from words at the ends of lines: *tomorrow, day, time, fools, candle, poor player, upon the stage, a tale, sound and fury, signifying nothing.*

Another great writer, William Faulkner, recognized in "sound and fury" a perfect title for one of his most famous novels, in part a tale told by an "idiot." These days we might call Faulkner's character Benjy Compson cognitively disabled. In *The Sound and the Fury* he is the first of four narrators, delivering his nonlinear view of the world in stream-of-consciousness prose considered revolutionary in its day. Ironically, it is a familiar literary move to have the tale told by the "village idiot" turn out to be the licensed truth.

Perhaps in my senescence I will teach a semester course on those ten lines from Macbeth: each week devoted to one line.

There is so much to see if you are wearing your X-ray glasses:

- all the words that define, mention, or measure time
- the repetition of words — even simple words like *and* — that have a ticktock quality to them, signifying the passage of time
- the contrast between images of darkness and light
- the alliterations in *petty* and *pace, dusty* and *death, tale* and *told, sound* and *signifying*
- the words that refer to language, writing, and story-telling, such as *syllable, recorded, tale*
- the self-referential allusion to stagecraft

In the end, what does it all signify? Nothing. Everything.

WRITING LESSONS

1. When you are drafting a passage, ask yourself this question: What is my most important or interesting element? Underline it. Now that you know what is important, try to emphasize that importance for the reader. Consider whether it can fit at the beginning or end of a passage — for emphasis.

2. If you prefer to *write* your way — rather than *plan* your way — to certain effects, go ahead and write a draft

without any conscious attention to word order. The best thing you can then do, my fellow writers, is examine your draft and underline the language that turns up at the ends of sentences and paragraphs. Those are the potential hot spots in your story. Make sure a great phrase is not hiding somewhere in the middle. If you find one, drag it out into the light, where we can all see it.

3. Titles are one of the most important elements of stories—arguably *the* most important. Why? Because many people decide whether to read a work based on its title. The original title of the adventure story *Treasure Island* by Robert Louis Stevenson was *The Sea-Cook*. Nice revision! We've seen here how William Faulkner borrowed a phrase from Shakespeare for the title of one of his most famous novels, *The Sound and the Fury*. Shakespeare is a great source for titles, but so are many other important works of literature. Just remember that when you borrow a phrase for your title, everything that is attached to that phrase, including the themes of the original story, come with it.

16

X

X-raying Shakespeare's Sonnets
Shaking the Form

One of the things I've liked best about writing this book is relearning literary lessons from my past. I was blessed with great English teachers in high school, college, and graduate school. Some of their lessons, which I may have dismissed at the time, have come back and put me in a hammerlock. The cool part, though, is that a student never has to settle for a teacher's X-ray reading of a famous text. You get to put on your own prescription pair of X-ray specs, seeing a text through your teacher's eyes and then looking down deeper.

T. S. Eliot and many other critics have written about the relationship between an individual author—let's be more specific: an individual poet—and the tradition of poetry that he or she inherits. No matter how rebellious, the poet has to account for what has come before. No matter how dismissive of traditional norms, that poet will leave traces of the past in his poetry, even if he treats these norms as radioactive.

The great sports journalist Red Smith once testified that his own writing style had changed over the course of four decades as he was able to slough off the influence of earlier, more ornate sportswriters in favor of a clear, authentic style. Smith compared it to the way that young athletes study the moves of older ones: they imitate those moves, master them, and take them to a new level. So you might see in a prize-fighter such as Sugar Ray Leonard the influence of a Muhammad Ali, who was himself influenced by the graceful and powerful Sugar Ray Robinson.

THE BIG MOVE

So here is a big writing move: study the moves of writers you admire (and some you don't). Without plagiarizing, look for ways to imitate that work. Be attentive to the way your own writing begins to show this influence and then moves beyond it.

A most instructive way to learn this literary choreography is to revisit the history of the English sonnet and study the ways in which Renaissance poets inherited a strict tradition of love poetry and reimagined it for a new generation of readers. From Sidney to Spenser to Shakespeare and beyond, the sonnet remained fourteen lines in length, but it acquired different stanza structures and rhyme schemes. It should not surprise us that no one was more nimble with the form than

Shakespeare, who demonstrated for the ages not one but two ways to shake up the box of traditional metaphors for love.

The two forms of rebellion are each represented best by a particular sonnet: number 18 and number 130. The first of these two is written to the poet's unnamed patron, a young man, idealized in the sonnets for his beauty and vitality:

> Shall I compare thee to a summer's day?
> Thou art more lovely and more temperate.
> Rough winds do shake the darling buds of May,
> And summer's lease hath all too short a date.
> Sometime too hot the eye of heaven shines,
> And often is his gold complexion dimmed;
> And every fair from fair sometime declines,
> By chance or nature's changing course untrimmed.
> But thy eternal summer shall not fade
> Nor lose possession of that fair thou ow'st,
> Nor shall Death brag thou wand'rest in his shade,
> When in eternal lines to time thou grow'st.
> > So long as men can breathe or eyes can see,
> > So long lives this, and this gives life to thee.

This sonnet is so famous and accessible that my mother, who at the age of ninety-five was losing her short-term memory, could recite the top of the poem without a problem. She memorized it as a high school student at Washington Irving High School, in New York City, in the 1930s.

The logic of the poem is straightforward: it would not be a good thing to compare a lover to a summer's day—a common comparison—because a summer's day can have imperfections. These metaphorical flaws of summer do not exist in the lover. The lover has a quality that a single day lacks—an "eternal summer" that "shall not fade." That immortality comes not from supernatural power but from the "eternal lines" of the poet. Every time this poem is read, the beauty and youth of the lover are resurrected: "So long as men can breathe or eyes can see, / So long lives this, and this gives life to thee." It is worth saying that more than four hundred years after Shakespeare wrote those lines, they are still true.

If I had to distill the rebellious argument of the poem in a sentence, it might go like this: "The standard metaphors to describe you are inadequate to the task; you are better than that." But where did those standard metaphors come from? One source was an Italian poet named Petrarch, who died in 1374 but who is associated with a style of love poetry that influenced the Italian and English Renaissance. By the time this tradition reached England, it had generated a list of standard metaphors associated with an idealized lover and forms of unrequited love.

In the standard catalog, the lover has a fair complexion, rosy cheeks, and blond hair (in twenty-first-century terms, think of a young Gwyneth Paltrow rather than a mature Angelina Jolie). Her breath is sweet, her voice like a song, her eyes as blue as the sea, her movement so light she seems to be floating in air. But because the consummation of the love is impossible, the unrequited lover must remain in agony. He wants to die. His tears fill an ocean. His sighs are like a tempest. So pervasive are these metaphors that they persist to this day—centuries after their conception—in the language of romance novels and cheesy greeting cards.

PLAYING WITH TRADITION

Shakespeare himself recognized how silly were the Petrarchan metaphors, if taken literally, and he offers a kind of parody in sonnet 130, one of a group of poems directed not to the youthful male patron but to a mysterious figure who has come down to us only as the Dark Lady:

> My mistress' eyes are nothing like the sun;
> Coral is far more red than her lips' red;
> If snow be white, why then her breasts are dun;
> If hairs be wires, black wires grow on her head.
> I have seen roses damasked, red and white,
> But no such roses see I in her cheeks;
> And in some perfumes is there more delight
> Than in the breath that from my mistress reeks.
> I love to hear her speak, yet well I know
> That music hath a far more pleasing sound.
> I grant I never saw a goddess go;
> My mistress, when she walks, treads on the ground.
> > And yet, by heaven, I think my love as rare
> > As any she belied with false compare.

I'm not sure Shakespeare wrote a funnier poem. It has a brilliant compare-contrast structure, in which a Petrarchan metaphor is suggested, then disposed of:

- Eyes like the sun? Not.
- Lips like coral? Not quite.
- Breasts as white as snow? Dun = "a slightly brownish dark gray."
  - Presumably gold wires for hair? How about black wires?
  - Cheeks like roses? Nope.
  - Breath like perfume? Hers reeks.
  - Voice like music? Not on his hit parade.
  - Floats like a goddess? Walks on the ground.

This demythologizing of love metaphors is remarkable for its thoroughness. The evidence is complete. But let's also hold it up against the argument of sonnet 18. There Shakespeare refuses to use another Petrarchan standard, the comparison of the lover to a perfect summer day, not because that metaphor is too good but because it is inadequate. It fails to measure up to the lover.

In sonnet 130 the metaphors are also no good, but for a different reason: they exaggerate the reality of the lover, holding her up against a false and ridiculous and unnatural standard. The patron is an idealized man, but the Dark Lady is a real woman. She treads on the ground. The poet loves her *because* of that: "And yet, by heaven, I think my love as rare / As any she belied with false compare." If you had to articulate a theme or topic for this sonnet, you could do no better than Shakespeare's final two words: "false compare"—that is, the lie of the false comparison, the exaggerated metaphor.

Throughout the history of the sonnet—Italian and English—there has been experimentation in rhyme scheme and stanza structure. In both our sonnets, Shakespeare builds an argument in the first eight lines that is answered in the final six. Each sonnet ends with a couplet: a rhyme that closes the door on the poem with a final, persuasive declaration. Let's X-ray sonnet 18:

> So long as men can breathe or eyes can see,
> So long lives this, and this gives life to thee.

- Notice first the repetition of the phrase "So long" at the top of each line.
- Notice that each line has ten words, and that each word is one syllable.
- Notice in that first line how the stress falls on key words (*long, men, breathe, eyes, see*), while the unstressed syllables are function words (*so, as, can, or, can*).
- Notice the alliterative word cluster: *long, lives, life.*
- Notice the parallel between "men can breathe" and "eyes can see."
- Notice the rhyme between *see* and *thee.*

This is hard work for two lines of poetry, but that's the point of the couplet ending a sonnet. Journalists have a word for an effective ending to a story. They call it a kicker, a word that may derive from the days of vaudeville, when performers would dance their way off the stage in a kick line. For Shakespeare, the couplet is a kicker for the sonnet.

It serves even better in that way in sonnet 130:

> And yet, by heaven, I think my love as rare
> As any she belied with false compare.

Notice how "And yet" serves as a tidy transition from the litany of seemingly negative comments about the lady.

LEARNING FROM SHAKESPEARE

Remember the "big writing move" I mentioned early in this chapter? To grow as a writer, you should read the works of writers you admire and look for ways to imitate that work. Over time the influence of that work will begin to fade, and your distinctive style will shine through.

When I wrote that advice, little did I realize I would soon be applying it to myself. As she approached her wedding day in 2014, my daughter Lauren looked for a reading for the ceremony. She was working in musical theater, and her fiancé was a professional musician, so her goal was to find a poem that used music as a metaphor for love. Nothing she found quite fit. So, having recently read a collection of Shakespeare's sonnets, I sat down with a green spiral notebook and gave it a shot. The final version looked like this:

Wedding Band
(A sonnet for Lauren and Chaż)

Every bride and groom should sing a song
Right before that time they say their words.
He could sing the bass notes deep and strong,
And she could trill the alto like a bird.

But what if he starts croaking like a frog,
And she can only buzz it like a bug?

Would we prefer the howling of a dog
To this unsound cacophony of love?

No, I say, just let the lovers sing!
It need not be in harmony or tune,
It need not turn like gold into a ring
Or squeeze exquisite honey from the moon.

It's the *trying* that's important — hand in hand —
Two voices circled join this wedding band.

At the risk of X-raying my own work (and being shocked at what I find), let me trace some direct and indirect influences from my experience of immersion in Shakespeare. While my sonnet is written in modern English and in a casual tone, I see these echoes of influence:

- a structure of fourteen lines
- a rhythm of iambic pentameter
- a similar rhyme scheme
- three stanzas of four lines each, followed by a couplet

The tone I strike here feels like a combination of the two that dominate the Bard's work. It takes the union of two lovers seriously, yet there is an intended humor that suggests that true love not only conquers imperfection but requires it. I am not an experienced poet, but I could still feel the energy and creativity that flowed through me from the playfulness of language. My wordplay was confined only by the limitations of nature and the poetic form. Chaz is a bass player in a great band called the Hunks of Funk, and Lauren is an alto in musical theater, so both those elements appear in the poem. More fun was the discovery of the adjective *unsound,* the double meaning of *wedding band,* the euphony of *squeeze* and *exquisite,* and the way in which the verb *join* carries marital connotations.

If it feels as if I am patting myself on the back for a mediocre poem, so be it. I am no Tiger Woods, but I derive great pleasure from sinking a long putt for a birdie. I am no Jerry Lee Lewis, but I feel transformed when playing my own version of "Great Balls of Fire." I am no Shakespeare, but I used his sweet influence to please my daughter and son-in-law on one of the most important days of their lives. Good enough.

WRITING LESSONS

1. Incorporate the reading of poetry into your habits of language learning. If any form of discourse was meant for X-ray reading, it is the poem, with its beautiful compression of language, meaning, and emotion.

2. Try your hand at writing poetry. If the sonnet seems too exacting a form, try something simpler—a haiku, for example. Counting syllables (five-seven-five for the haiku) is a great way to get started. Don't think of this process as disconnected from your other, more practical work as a writer. The headline, for example, is a compressed form of writing. So is the tweet, with its 140-character length. Forms of writing connect with one another in both mundane and mysterious ways.

3. Use your X-ray reading skills to study and understand the traditions in which some forms of writing exist: from the sonnet to the novel, from the ship's log to the Web log. Pay special attention to the parts that create the structure of the work. Learn the names of those parts.

4. Poetry begs to be read aloud, but so does great prose. When you come across a piece of writing that moves you in a special way, you can use two strategies to intensify that experience. First, you can read the passage aloud. Read it aloud to yourself, then read it to another person, then let another person read it to you. You can also type out the prose, getting the sense of what it feels like to re-create it with your own fingers.

5. Remember the big move. Study writers you admire and imitate them without plagiarizing. Over time, play with that influence to find your own voice, just as Shakespeare played with the form of the sonnet.

17

X

X-raying *Moby-Dick*

Three Little Words

I have a vague recollection of reading—or at least perusing—a children's version of the book *Moby-Dick* as a boy. That experience left me with two indelible memories. The first was of Captain Ahab and his wooden leg, a prosthetic limb that was required after a whale bit off the captain's real leg. The idea of some monstrous sea creature crunching down on a human limb added a creep factor to the yarn that attracted the attention of a ten-year-old boy. The second involved the whale itself, big enough to sink a ship and albino in its appearance. Usually black serves as the color of darkness, but in this tale it is the reversal of that expectation that leaves even more creep in its wake. For a kid, the character of Moby Dick prefigured the toothy monsters of movies such as *Piranha*, *Jaws*, and the best worst movie ever made, *Sharknado*.

The great literary critic Leslie Fiedler once noted that it has been a mark of early American literature that serious works with adult themes have been consigned too often to the ranks of kid lit. "Rip Van Winkle," "The Legend of Sleepy Hollow," *The Last of the Mohicans, The Adventures of Huckleberry Finn,* and, yes, *Moby-Dick* once suffered that fate — at least at a time when boys were still reading literature at all. It takes only a bit of X-ray reading to see the fallacy that Fiedler describes. *Moby-Dick,* our current example, is an adult book from the first three words on. By the end of the first paragraph, the reader is ready to call a shrink. By the end of the book, something both profound and transcendental has occurred. When I read *Moby-Dick* in college, it felt like a work that couldn't decide whether it wanted to be a whaling manual or a gothic novel. By graduate school it had the weight of scripture.

Here's the beginning of that first paragraph:

Call me Ishmael. Some years ago — never mind how long precisely — having little or no money in my purse, and nothing particular to interest me on shore, I thought I would sail about a little and see the watery part of the world. It is a way I have of driving off the spleen, and regulating the circulation. Whenever I find myself growing grim about the mouth; whenever it is a damp, drizzly November in my soul; whenever I find myself involuntarily pausing before coffin warehouses, and bringing up the rear of every funeral I meet; and especially whenever my hypos get such an upper hand of me, that it requires a strong moral principle to prevent me from deliberately

stepping into the street, and methodically knocking people's hats off—then, I account it high time to get to sea as
soon as I can.

There is a lot going on in that passage of 145 words, a great
well of words that writers can draw from. If anything, the
final 142 words have suffered, tiny fish swimming aimlessly
behind that great three-word whale of a first sentence, a
phrase that has become part of our literary culture, quoted
or parodied countless times in criticism, literature, and
popular culture: "Call me Ishmael."

(A digression will do you good. In the early 1980s, I par-
ticipated in a conference on journalism standards and practices in which I concluded my remarks with these two short
sentences: "Call me irresponsible. Call me Ishmael." The
conference was recorded and then transcribed, and the poor
transcriber must have skipped nineteenth-century American literature in college, because when I read her transcript
it turned out as: "Call me irresponsible. Call me a schmuck."
"Ishmael" became "a schmuck." Don't you feel better?)

SHORT SENTENCE AS GOSPEL

"Call me Ishmael." What makes that a perfect sentence? I
can make a list:

1. It is a short, short sentence within a long, long novel.
2. It introduces the first-person narrator.
3. It has an oddly potent structure, not the standard
   subject, verb, object. When I tried to decipher the

syntax, the best I could come up with was imperative verb, indirect object, and I haven't the foggiest idea. The experts at LanguageLog.com steered me toward "verb, direct object, and [the always popular] predicate complement."

4. The sentence has some mystery to it. The narrator doesn't give you his real name, and you wonder why.

5. It introduces a biblical allusion — one that points to an outcast, alienated son.

That is so much work done so efficiently. Author Tom Wolfe once argued that when readers confront a short, short sentence, they treat it as the gospel truth. At the Poynter Institute we call this the "Jesus wept" effect, a reference to one of the shortest sentences in the Bible. When Jesus returns home to discover that his cousin Lazarus has died, his response is profoundly human. Many who may doubt the miracle of Jesus raising Lazarus from the dead are less likely to doubt this moment: "Jesus wept." The simple power of two words — subject and verb — should encourage us to cast our most important ideas in the shortest possible sentences.

ARC OF THE ARK

Before we crown Melville's first sentence and first paragraph as champions, we'd best look at the novel's ending, because, as was the case with *Gatsby,* the greatest beginnings can have in them the seeds of the greatest endings. Previous to these final paragraphs, the whale kills the monomaniacal Ahab and destroys his ship and his crew — except for one sailor:

The drama's done. Why then here does any one step forth?——Because one did survive the wreck.

....So, floating on the margin of the ensuing scene, and in full sight of it, when the halfspent suction of the sunk ship reached me, I was then, but slowly, drawn towards the closing vortex. When I reached it, it had subsided to a creamy pool. Round and round, then, and ever contracting towards the button-like black bubble at the axis of that slowly wheeling circle, like another Ixion I did revolve. Till, gaining that vital centre, the black bubble upward burst; and now, liberated by reason of its cunning spring, and, owing to its great buoyancy, rising with great force, the coffin life-buoy shot lengthwise from the sea, fell over, and floated by my side. Buoyed up by that coffin, for almost one whole day and night, I floated on a soft and dirgelike main. The unharming sharks, they glided by as if with padlocks on their mouths; the savage sea-hawks sailed with sheathed beaks. On the second day, a sail drew near, nearer, and picked me up at last. It was the devious-cruising Rachel, that in her retracing search after her missing children, only found another orphan.

Hmm...where have we seen that coffin before?

ALLUSION, NOT ILLUSION

I've argued that all authors need backup singers to make their points. Gladys Knight was at her best with her Pips. In nonfiction these backup singers can be sources of information who are quoted to provide evidence. In fiction they may be characters who speak to the readers on behalf of the author. Sometimes they arrive in the form of a literary or cultural allusion—figures who bring their own old stories to bear on the new one, an effect with the technical name intertextuality, a concept we'll explore in depth in chapter 25.

In the reference to Ixion, Melville alludes to a villainous king from Greek mythology whom Zeus punished by placing him on a fiery wheel that rotated forever. But Ishmael is no villain, and though he spins on a watery wheel, he will not be sucked into the vortex.

The biblical character of Ishmael is introduced in the book of Genesis. He is the firstborn son of Abraham, the product of his union with the handmaiden Hagar. When the wife of Abraham, Sarah, has a child, Ishmael becomes expendable, and he spends his life wandering in the desert. That story turns him into an alienated son, a displaced orphan. Just as Melville replaces the fiery wheel of Ixion with a wheel of water, he replaces the biblical desert of Ishmael with a watery wasteland.

It is fitting, then, that the name of the ship that rescues Ishmael is the *Rachel*. The mother of the Jewish patriarchs Joseph and Benjamin, Rachel is described in the book of Jeremiah as "Rachel weeping for her children." The children in this context are the people of Israel punished by a jealous God and condemned to wander through the desert without a homeland.

COFFIN AS LIFEBOAT

And how does the ship *Rachel* find her orphaned child Ishmael? In a coffin, of course, turned into a lifeboat. By now, it should not surprise us that this brilliant narrative inversion—the container of death turned into a vessel of life—is foreshadowed in *Moby-Dick*'s second sentence. Remember this? "Whenever I find myself involuntarily pausing before coffin warehouses, and bringing up the rear of every funeral I meet…"

Once again we discover that wonderful pattern in classic and popular literature that goes something like this: "Look for those moments when a curse becomes a blessing and a blessing becomes a curse." In Christian theology, the loss of paradise by Adam and Eve becomes known as the *felix culpa*, the happy fault, because it paves the way for Christ, the savior. Poor Rudolph the Red-Nosed Reindeer is ostracized from reindeer games until his incandescent proboscis helps Santa through the foggy night. In the Harry Potter stories, the teacher Harry hates most—Severus Snape—becomes his greatest protector and benefactor. For Ishmael, a product of that coffin factory—a sign of his melancholy and landlocked ennui—becomes a life buoy, a means of rescue that provides our narrator, whose real name we never learn, with the chance to tell his story.

WRITING LESSONS

1. Read the Bible. This is not a plea for you to become religious—or more religious. But if you don't know the sto-

ries of the Bible and its main characters, you are cutting yourself off from the most powerful source of allusion in Western culture — with Shakespeare a distant second.

2. Embrace brevity. I've written a book about short writing, which may be a contradiction in terms. But short bits can accumulate. How many stones does it take to build a cathedral? Remember that this eight-hundred-page novel begins with a three-word sentence.

3. Learn the name. Nonfiction writers gather interesting names. Fiction writers can invent them. Names become part of character development, but they also send messages about class, culture, race, region, nationality, and history.

4. Offer mystery. Two words I love to use in my writing are "mystery" and "secret." Readers will make a journey with you if you help them solve a mystery or expose a secret. The great white whale and Captain Ahab's obsession with it contain mysteries and secrets, but so does the first sentence. Who is this man who would have you call him Ishmael?

5. Foreshadow. Can you imagine writing a story in which a word in the first paragraph saves the life of the hero in the last? Look at the way a death box — a coffin — in the beginning becomes a lifeboat in the end.

18

X

X-raying W. B. Yeats
Sacred Center

I don't know how many words were written by Ireland's most famous poet, William Butler Yeats, but I begin this chapter by X-raying a single word. It comes at the end of the first line of one of his most well-known poems, "The Second Coming." The word is *gyre,* and the line is: "Turning and turning in the widening gyre."

My plan is to draw at least three writing strategies from that single word:

1. Never be afraid to use an unfamiliar word, even one that your readers might not understand.

2. If you think a strange word will not be understood, create a context to guide the reader toward meaning.

3. Before you use such a word, consult various dictionaries to discover its literal and figurative meanings, its connotations, and its history and language of origin.

I have never used the word *gyre* in my prose and did not even know how to pronounce it before X-raying this poem. But I now know a lot because I followed strategy number 3, which is not only for writers but also for advanced X-ray readers. If you read a passage and want to know what makes it work, you must drill down into individual phrases, words, and even letters and marks of punctuation. Meaning is created in reading and writing by the subtlest gestures of language.

WORD AT WORK

So I have consulted a number of dictionaries to understand *gyre,* and here are some of the things I've learned:

- The word is a noun, but it can also be a verb.
- All its meanings and associations have something to do with turning.
- Its literal meaning is "a circular or spiral form; a vortex."
- Synonyms, besides *vortex,* include *maelstrom* and *whirlpool* (like the one at the end of *Moby-Dick*!).
- A gyre can describe a powerful force in the air or at sea.
- It rhymes with *lyre* and *wire* and is pronounced as two syllables: "ji-er," with emphasis on the first.

- The *g* is soft, like the first sound in the word *jump*.
- *Gyre* derives from the Greek word *guros,* meaning "circle."
- It shares that etymology with other surprising words:

Gyrate: "to revolve around a fixed point or axis," as a stripper around a pole;

Gyroscope: "a device consisting of a spinning mass," used to help vehicles maintain correct balance and orientation;

Gyro: "a sandwich made usually of sliced roasted lamb" — a reference to meat turning on a spit.

In each case, the movement in a circle requires a strong, fixed center.

With that as background, let's X-ray the first stanza of "The Second Coming," eight lines consisting of fifty-three words:

Turning and turning in the widening gyre
The falcon cannot hear the falconer;
Things fall apart; the centre cannot hold;
Mere anarchy is loosed upon the world,
The blood-dimmed tide is loosed, and everywhere
The ceremony of innocence is drowned;
The best lack all conviction, while the worst
Are full of passionate intensity. ——

This is a poem about politics, inspired, no doubt, by cat- aclysmic events such as World War I, the Irish rebellion against the British, and the Russian Revolution. Yeats and his generation of writers saw much violence, many deaths, many countries in ruins, and the social contract in tatters. In the line "Mere anarchy is loosed upon the world," *mere* means "total."

ACTION WORDS

The image in the first two lines is that of a falconer trying to control a falcon, a fierce bird of prey. Falconry is a royal, aristocratic sport, and control of a falcon signifies the power that rulers once had in taming dark threats to the social order. At the center was the king, and all revolved around him, based upon his power and his whim. Thomas Hobbes described that force in *Leviathan:* without it, "the life of man [is] solitary, poor, nasty, brutish, and short."

So the falconer needs to exercise control, but Yeats gives us a falcon that is spinning higher and higher, no longer able to hear the voice of its master, essentially gaining altitude and achieving what rocket scientists call escape velocity.

Let's X-ray that remarkable first line, which begins "Turning and turning." How interesting to begin a poem with a repeated word in the form of present participles. The repetition and those "ing" endings signify recurring action. Another "ing" word follows: *widening,* that long vowel sound in the first syllable preparing us for the next word, *gyre.*

We can divide this line in two different ways. We can separate "Turning and turning" from "widening gyre," creating a kind of balance. Or we can look at it as a line of Anglo-Saxon poetry in which the first three key words connect, preparing the way for the final beat. *Turning, turning,* and *widening* each have more than one syllable, end with "ing," and denote action—leading to that short noun, *gyre,* at the end.

SUBTLE CHANGES IN LANGUAGE

Consider how an echo is achieved in the second line—not by an exact repetition of a word (as in *turning*) but rather by the juxtaposition of two almost identical words (*falcon* and *falconer*), with a small difference becoming a grand one. By analogy, a musician lowers the middle note in a triad by only a half step to turn a joyful major chord into a sorrowful minor one. "The falcon cannot hear the falconer." In many sentences the key words come at the beginning and the end, but here they come in the middle: "cannot hear."

These phrases are famous: "Things fall apart; the centre cannot hold," and the way they rub shoulders deserves close attention. "Things fall apart" feels like common speech, almost a cliché, the kind of broad generality you would speak to comfort one who has experienced a death in the family or a divorce. What's that? The Beatles are breaking up? Hell, things fall apart. This feels self-evident, a truism.

The second part seems less common and buttresses the first. It's a statement that has the feel of science in it, especially physics. The force is centrifugal, outward from the center, the opposite of centripetal. The reference is back to the falcon and its widening gyre. Anything out of control is a threat to the common good.

Like Hobbes, Yeats imagines the result of this loss of central control:

Mere anarchy is loosed upon the world,
The blood-dimmed tide is loosed, and everywhere
The ceremony of innocence is drowned;

I see a peculiar type of repetition in these three lines. The word *loosed* is repeated, in the sense of "being let loose." Think again of a falconer letting a falcon loose to fly but expecting to bring it back under his control. More interesting is the way that each line is expressed in the passive voice. The subjects (mere anarchy, the blood-dimmed tide, the ceremony of innocence) are all passive, receiving the action of some unknown terrible force in the universe. In classic literature this is a deus ex machina, a godlike force that arrives late in a story to solve the world's problems. For Yeats, it is not the Jesus of the Second Coming who brings salvation to the world. We learn in subsequent lines that Yeats imagines a sphinxlike monster, a "rough beast" that "Slouches towards Bethlehem to be born."

It should not surprise us that biblical references abound — as we saw with Joyce — from a writer raised in an Irish Catholic culture. The tide, which should be a blue-green cleansing force, is instead "blood-dimmed" from all the victims of war and revolution, suggesting one of the Ten Plagues of Egypt, in which God punished the pharaoh by turning the Nile to blood. The ceremony of innocence, a general reference to all the creative and positive trappings of civilization, also recalls the Slaughter of the Innocents, King Herod's response to prophecies of the birth of Jesus. The two lines, like all the humans sacrificed by God at the time of Noah and the Great Flood, converge at the word *drowned*.

SAY IT LIKE YOU MEAN IT

Such imagery paves the way for one of the most meaningful statements ever made about politics, culture, human society, and values:

> The best lack all conviction, while the worst
> Are full of passionate intensity.

It carries the weight of an aphorism—a short statement impossible to prove or disprove that has about it the ring of undeniable truth. This book is not about politics, but as I survey America and the world from my vantage point, Yeats's statement remains convincing. There is plenty of evidence of passionate intensity among the worst of us and lack of conviction in the rest of us. Yeats inspires me to be less hesitant in expressing the ideas I believe in. While I understand the importance of indirection in writing through irony, ambivalence, and ambiguity, I applaud those who marshal evidence to make a clear, convincing point. I am not encouraging pedantic lectures, self-righteous homilies, or ideological rants. But if you believe in a theme, a thesis, or even a topic sentence in a paragraph, write it loud and proud.

INVERTING THE FAMILIAR

Yeats remains a poet's poet, the kind of writer whose spirit is tapped by other writers of all kinds for its music and meaning. I know that my old friend Howell Raines kept a copy of Yeats's poetry close at hand, and he dipped into it each morning—close to his cup of coffee, I imagine—to kick-start his creative day.

Irish Catholicism has been a powerful cultural and political force, not just in Ireland but in the United States as well. In its most conservative form, it can be surprisingly puritanical. There are countless parochial schoolchildren who can testify to their experiences under the dominating influence of Catholic nuns and priests. There is rich tradition in this experience—beauty, music, and scholarship that are the glory of the world. But there is also rebellion and sin and drunkenness and the Troubles, which led to years of sectarian strife in Northern Ireland. And then there is the terrible scandal of sexual abuse of children by priests, whose fallibility and hypocrisy shook the foundations of one of the world's great religions.

James Joyce escaped Ireland and wrote of it from the Continent. Yeats stayed put but abandoned Roman Catholicism for arguably even more occult forms and rituals of spirituality, which are described in this poem. Even nonbelievers are imprinted with the fiery brand of the culture.

Consider his title, "The Second Coming." It denotes the religious belief that Christ will return triumphantly to the earth at some undetermined "omega point" in the future. No one refers specifically to the "first coming," the birth of Jesus, the son of God, in Bethlehem. The poet's Second Coming points not to the Christian final days but to a much darker apocalypse. A cynic might interpret the title and the poem that follows as a bait and switch—Christian imagery that turns pagan. Most critics see Yeats's title as something more brilliant and benevolent: the adaptation and reimagining of a powerful phrase, fraught with connotations, at a time when the answers supplied by Christianity and other great religions no longer seemed adequate to the plight of human beings.

WRITING LESSONS

1. Never be afraid to use an unfamiliar word, such as *gyre,* even one that your readers might not understand. If you think a strange word will not be understood, create a context to guide the reader toward meaning.

2. Repeating a word in close proximity—as in "down, down" and "slow, slow"—creates the effect of continuous action. Words can be linked together by repetition, as in the vowel sounds of *widening* and *gyre* and in the endings of *turning* and *widening.* Words that end in "ing" contribute to that sense of continuous action.

3. Simple and common words can be used to generate the most powerful ideas, as in "Things fall apart; the centre cannot hold." Yeats uses the semicolon as a swinging gate, a mark that separates equal elements, but he lets the reader pass from one to the other.

4. Stick to your guns. Don't be afraid to make a statement, as in "The best lack all conviction." As Tom Wolfe advises, short statements and sentiments have the feel of gospel truth.

5. Don't be afraid to surprise readers by frustrating their expectations. Choose a common phrase or symbol, such as "the Second Coming," and repurpose it for a radically different interpretation.

19

X

X-raying Zora Neale Hurston
Words on Fire

The 2014 release of a hot trailer for the movie version of *Fifty Shades of Grey* stirred up renewed attention to the book trilogy that spawned it, the work of a lucky British woman named E. L. James. I like the arc of her personal story: from self-publishing the first book to sales of more than ninety million copies worldwide, with translations into more than fifty languages. So perhaps I should make this a short chapter with a single piece of advice to writers: sex sells.

But just as there is good food writing and bad food writing, good sportswriting and bad sportswriting, there is also good sex writing and bad sex writing. To illustrate this, I have chosen a scene—almost at random—from one of James's books to X-ray. As you will see, it turns out to be much less graphic than the bondage scenes for which her work has become notorious, but the style of writing remains consistent:

> Christian nods as he turns and leads me through the double doors into the grandiose foyer. I revel in the feel of his large hand and his long, skilled fingers curled around mine. I feel the familiar pull—I am drawn, Icarus to his sun. I have been burned already, and yet here I am again.
>
> Reaching the elevators, he presses the call button. I peek up at him, and he's wearing his enigmatic half smile. As the doors open, he releases my hand and ushers me in. The doors close and I risk a second peek. He glances down at me, gray eyes alive, and it's there in the air between us, that electricity. It's palpable. I can almost taste it, pulsing between us, drawing us together.
>
> "Oh my," I gasp as I bask briefly in the intensity of this visceral, primal attraction.
>
> "I feel it, too," he says, his eyes clouded and intense.
>
> Desire pools dark and deadly in my groin. He clasps my hand and grazes my knuckles with his thumb, and all my muscles clench tightly, deliciously, deep inside me.
>
> *Holy cow. How can he still do this to me?*
>
> "Please don't bite your lip, Anastasia," he whispers.
>
> I gaze up at him, releasing my lip. I want him. Here, now, in the elevator. How could I not?
>
> "You know what it does to me," he murmurs.
>
> Oh, I still affect him. My inner goddess stirs from her five-day sulk.

Oy. What I usually call X-ray reading must briefly devolve into *sex*-ray reading.

There is nothing original or interesting or even mildly erotic about this passage. We've seen or heard it all before: Icarus flying too close to the sun. (When I saw that, I blurted out, "Oh, not Icarus again. See what you've done, Stephen Dedalus? Can't we find another, less abused mythological figure?") The encounter in the elevator is a staple in everything from porn movies to TV commercials. What follows are those suspiciously large hands and long fingers. There are those coy glances, and electricity in the air between them. Can you imagine that? Electricity in the air between them—in an elevator? (Does that mean a short circuit in the fuse box?) There must be pulsing—don't forget the pulsing. Add some gasping and basking, and let's not forget a bit of the visceral and primal. There is clasping and clenching and grazing. No mommy porn can be complete without the appearance of the word *deep*. The closest thing to original language is "Desire pools dark and deadly in my groin." But all that alliteration cannot muffle the screams in my head that protest against the collision of *pools* and *groin*. Is this passion, I wonder, or a urinary tract infection?

EROTIC VERSUS PORNOGRAPHIC

To neutralize the poison of this passage, I offer a counterexample, also written by a woman, Florida's own Zora Neale Hurston. *Their Eyes Were Watching God* was published in 1937 to mixed and controversial reviews but is now counted among the important novels of the twentieth century. A blurb by Alice Walker on the seventy-fifth-anniversary edition reads: "There is no book more important to me than this one."

A photo of a pear tree appears on the cover, and beneath the title, an image of a bee. That artwork pays homage to the book's most famous passage. The main character, Janie Crawford, thinks back to when she was sixteen years old. Her memories of a young lover, Johnny Taylor, turn into an erotic reverie.

It was a spring afternoon in West Florida. Janie had spent most of the day under a blossoming pear tree in the back-yard. She had been spending every minute that she could steal from her chores under that tree for the last three days. That was to say, ever since the first tiny bloom had opened. It had called her to come and gaze on a mystery. From barren brown stems to glistening leaf-buds; from the leaf-buds to snowy virginity of bloom. It stirred her tremendously....

She was stretched on her back beneath the pear tree soaking in the alto chant of the visiting bees, the gold of the sun and the panting breath of the breeze when the inaudible voice of it all came to her. She saw a dust-bearing bee sink into the sanctum of a bloom; the thousand sister-calyxes arch to meet the love embrace and the ecstatic shiver of the tree from root to tiniest branch creaming in every blossom and frothing with delight. So this was a marriage! She had been summoned to behold a revelation. Then Janie felt a pain remorseless sweet that left her limp and languid....

Through pollinated air she saw a glorious being coming up the road. In her former blindness she had known him as shiftless Johnny Taylor, tall and lean. That was before the golden dust of pollen had beglamored his rags and her eyes.

Are your X-ray glasses steaming up? You don't need them to realize that this passage is a highly stylized description of a sexualized sensibility. Let's hear it for sex. I'm all for sex — in life and literature. I've studied the ways human sexuality is portrayed in popular culture and in art. You would think that decades of such contemplation would lead to wisdom, but I admit to being as confused as ever about the power that sex holds over us. Only religion can compete. Sex, beyond its biological imperatives, is a cultural force that fascinates us, dominates our thinking, and drives us to act in ways that help us, hurt us, and complicate our lives.

Descriptions and depictions of sex in media, advertising, literature, and drama, I would argue, are easy enough to create but difficult to do well.

Let's consider the difference between creative work that is *erotic* versus work that is *pornographic*. My inclination is to identify pornography by what it says and erotica by what it does not say. Porn is, in practice if not by definition, prone to exaggeration and overstatement; eros works by suggestion, imagery, and understatement. Both porn and eros have the same desired effect: to excite the body, to prepare it for sex.

Porn does this primarily through the eyes; eros through the imagination.

What interests me most about Hurston's passage—beyond its erotic allure—is the way in which the most standard metaphors of language are transformed from common and euphemistic into astonishing and exciting.

To use the most old-fashioned language, a woman who loses her virginity is said to be "deflowered." When young teens begin to learn about sexuality, it's all about "the birds and the bees." The parts of a flower, we might have learned in high school biology, have their male and female equivalents. We can find traces of all these comparisons in Hurston's passage, yet the power and originality of the language unveils the sex act in ways we haven't seen before.

Sometimes a pear tree, Dr. Freud, is more than a pear tree.

There is a name for Hurston's technique, and as an anthropologist and author, she would have known it: anthropomorphism. Here's the definition from *The American Heritage Dictionary:* "attribution of human motivation, characteristics, or behavior to inanimate objects, animals, or natural phenomena." This process is easy enough to recognize when the subject is a mammal or primate but becomes harder as we move down the chain of being. When it's a flower, Hurston gives its bloom a "snowy virginity." The breeze has a "breath" and even "pants" like an energetic lover. There is a "love embrace" and even a "marriage" between the parts of the tree.

Then there is a cluster of words and images that in a different context or via expressions of connotation reminds us of sexuality. A tree blossoms and blooms; so, in a sense, does a young woman. Janie is "stretched on her back beneath the pear tree" as if it were her lover. A bee will "sink into the sanctum of a bloom," bearing pollen and carrying countless associations with sexual union, fertility, and procreation. The "thousand sister-calyxes" are the sepals of a group of flowers, but "calyx" also describes the cuplike structure of the human anatomy, such as a pelvis. It arches, as a lover would arch her back, and the result is a kind of orgasm: "the ecstatic shiver of the tree from root to tiniest branch creaming in every blossom and frothing with delight." (In porn, that's called the money shot.) At the end of that passage, Janie is a spent lover, feeling "limp and languid," alliterative words beginning with liquid consonants that offer their own kind of lubrication.

What a great change of perspective to look down a road through the glorious haze of "pollinated air" and see the human object of Janie's desire. He is transformed now through the lens of her sex-ray vision: "the golden dust of pollen had beglamored his rags and her eyes." There is magic at work here. The pollen is a form of fairy dust. To be "beglamored" means to be transformed as if in a spell or trance.

LANGUAGE OF LOVE

To understand how good this is—how artful and controlled— all that is needed is to contrast it to *Fifty Shades of Grey*.

The key to writing good sex (good anything) is original language. Consider how Vladimir Nabokov describes Humbert Humbert's first sighting of Dolores Haze, who would become his beloved Lolita. That vision would remind him of a lost love from long ago:

> With awe and delight…I saw again her lovely indrawn abdomen where my southbound mouth had briefly paused; and those puerile hips on which I had kissed the crenulated imprint left by the band of her shorts…. The twenty-five years I had lived since then tapered to a palpitating point, and vanished.

At one point early in the novel Humbert laments, "Oh, my Lolita, I only have words to play with!" Rather than a lament, Nabokov could adopt it as a boast, for I know no other novelist who is as relentlessly playful with the English language. Enjoy some of the phrases above, especially the dyads "indrawn abdomen" and "southbound mouth"; "crenulated imprint" and "palpitating point." Appreciate the balance, alliteration, assonance, repetition, variation — the wild and witty texture of the prose.

Now hold it up against "Holy cow. How can he still do this to me?"

WRITING LESSONS

1. Indirection often has more power than direction. In an age of hard-core pornography, it may be difficult to remember that there was a time, not long ago, when a peek at a garter belt had sexual power (as acted out in the television series *Mad Men,* set in the 1960s). In an earlier century, it might have been the sight of a bare ankle. In an interview,

the great Lauren Bacall suggested to me that the movies she made in her youth were sexier than more explicit contemporary films because of what they suggested and left out.

2. Almost anything can be described symbolically, including violence, illness, and sexuality. There is more than a partridge in Hurston's pear tree. Human capacities and sensibilities can be used to describe animals, plants, even nonliving things. We name hurricanes, after all, and storms are said "to rage."

3. As George Orwell reminds us, avoid language you are used to seeing in print. Try to take standard or tired language to a next level. Hurston's brilliance derives from her ability to transform language and images that could be used as euphemisms for sexuality (bees and flowers) into something so vivid and original that it can almost be felt.

4. America manages to be a country that is both puritanical and pornographic in many of its cultural manifestations. In such a society, it's especially important to write boldly about sex acts and the consequences of sexual activity. It's also a good idea to find a test audience before publication to avoid the pitfalls of silliness or crude insensitivity. Try not to forget (gentlemen!) that sex can be experienced in the context of love. And, yes, it's true: sex sells. Get cooking.

20

X

X-raying Harper Lee
Weight of the Wait

There are certain days in a writer's life when the stars seem in alignment. As I was revising this chapter about *To Kill a Mockingbird* and the writing strategies of Harper Lee, news broke that her publisher will produce a sequel to *Mockingbird* entitled *Go Set a Watchman*. When it comes to suspenseful storytelling, there is nothing like a long wait followed by a big surprise.

Although it was published in 1960, during the classic period of the civil rights movement, *Mockingbird* is set in a small southern town during the Depression years 1933–35. Thanks to a movie version that won an Academy Award and book sales worldwide of more than eighteen million copies, the story is now familiar. A righteous Alabama lawyer and legislator, Atticus Finch (played by Gregory Peck in the movie), raises his son, Jem, and his daughter, Scout, with a progressive view of race and justice. In the segregated South, this turns out to be a daunting and even dangerous task, especially when Atticus is called to defend a black man accused of raping a white woman. The story is narrated by Scout, a spirited and determined child. Throughout the action the children find themselves mired in a series of misadventures. Their ingenuity and loyalty to their father gain them access to the courtroom, where they get to view the trial from the balcony. It is there where the black citizens of the town have gathered, hoping against hope for a just judgment for one of their own.

RHETORICAL GRAMMAR

I will focus my X-ray reading on chapter 21, not only the best and most revealing chapter in the book but also one of the best chapters in all of American literature. In the previous chapter, Atticus offers the jury a passionate summation, not only reviewing the evidence but also encouraging the all-white, all-male jury to follow their better angels:

> But there is one way in this country in which all men are created equal—there is one human institution that makes a pauper the equal of a Rockefeller, the stupid man the equal of an Einstein, and the ignorant man the equal of any college president. That institution, gentlemen, is a court. It can be the Supreme Court of the United States or the humblest J.P. [justice of the peace] court in the land, or this honorable court which you serve. Our courts have their faults, as does any human institution, but in this

country our courts are the great levelers, and in our courts all men are created equal.

I'm no idealist to believe firmly in the integrity of our courts and in the jury system — that is no ideal to me, it is a living, working reality. Gentlemen, a court is no better than each man of you sitting before me on this jury. A court is only as sound as its jury, and a jury is only as sound as the men who make it up. I am confident that you gentlemen will review without passion the evidence you have heard, come to a decision, and restore this defendant to his family. In the name of God, do your duty.

It's worth noting, through your X-ray glasses, how rhetorical this passage is. We know from Shakespeare that soliloquies — individual speeches to the audience — can enrich the experience of dramatic literature. A speech inside a story is another example of a text within a text, and it can be used to advance a story, reveal a character, or explore a set of ideas.

We can recognize again the familiar rhetorical strategies that make a passage feel like a powerful piece of oratory. One is the use of parallel constructions — repeated grammatical patterns. Look, for example, at this passage:

There is one human institution that makes a pauper the equal of a Rockefeller, the stupid man the equal of an Einstein, and the ignorant man the equal of any college president.

The word *equal* is repeated three times as an anchor, but all the other elements are varied — within a pattern. The rollout of three elements — Rockefeller, Einstein, college president — signifies that the speaker is making a broad, encompassing statement about the world. (Authors often use three examples as shorthand for "everything.")

It shouldn't surprise us that the speaker builds his language to a crescendo of passion and meaning and ends by invoking God and driving his listeners toward action, casting the most important sentiment within the shortest sentence, just eight words, seven of them in one syllable: "In the name of God, do your duty."

STORY ENGINES

By the beginning of chapter 21, the summation is concluded and the jury is about to begin its deliberations. Among the most familiar story engines is "guilty or not guilty." This is why jury trials make such popular dramatic narratives, from *Twelve Angry Men* to *Anatomy of a Murder* to countless episodes of *Perry Mason* and *Law and Order*. It also explains why the coverage of high-profile trials is a staple of cable news programs, most notably with the trial and acquittal of O. J. Simpson. Viewers will follow the proceedings for weeks and even months, not just to learn what has happened but also to find out what *will* happen. The rituals of trials, some of which can be most tedious, also have some suspense built into them — a system of delay, made more dramatic by jury deliberations, with the final outcome in doubt.

We will discover the verdict at the end of chapter 21, but not without a series of delays. In most ticktock structures either time is counted down, as in a basketball game, or it builds to a predetermined point, such as in the famous cowboy movie *High Noon,* whose title signifies the arrival time of a train carrying a killer named Frank Miller. The Miller gang will seek vengeance against the town and especially its marshal, played by Gary Cooper. The film is only eighty-five minutes long, and the action—measured by the hands of a large clock—occurs almost in real time.

Time, we know from experience and from quantum mechanics, is relative. In my personal theory of time, its speed depends on our consciousness of it. If we are "watching the clock" in a classroom or workplace, time can crawl. Or, if we are distracted by work or entertainment, it can "fly by." Where did the time go? we ask after a particularly engaging experience.

We might imagine, then, that to create suspense an author may want to slow down the narrative. This can be done by writing a series of short sentences, with each period acting as a stop sign. And it can be done by direct and repeated references to time. In *Mockingbird* we are awaiting a verdict. Jury deliberations, especially in the Jim Crow South, could be over in a few minutes. Or they could take days and days. Or the jury could be hung. What will happen? That's what the characters in the novel, and all its readers, want to find out.

TICKTOCK STRUCTURE

As chapter 21 begins, the family housekeeper, Calpurnia, has rushed into the courtroom, frantic with the news that the children, Jem and Scout, are missing and unaccounted for. The puzzle is quickly solved by the alert court reporter:

"I know where they are, Atticus. . . . They're right up yonder in the colored balcony—been there since precisely one-eighteen p.m."

There are two highly significant elements in this piece of dialogue. The first reminds us that in this segregated arena, the children sought refuge among the "colored" people. The other is the odd precision in the marking of time: "precisely one-eighteen p.m." Atticus agrees that they can return to the courthouse to hear the verdict, but he says that they must first go home, with an angry Calpurnia, and eat their supper. She serves them milk, potato salad, and ham, but insists, "You all eat slow," another reference to time.

When they return to the courthouse, Jem asks, about the jury, "How long have they been out?" Thirty minutes. After more waiting, Jem asks, "What time is it, Reverend?" He answers, "Gettin' on toward eight." More waiting. Then, "The old courthouse clock suffered its preliminary strain and struck the hour, eight deafening bongs that shook our bones." And then "When it bonged eleven times I was past feeling: tired from fighting sleep, I allowed myself a short nap against Reverend Sykes's comfortable arm and shoulder." More waiting. Scout addresses Jem:

"Ain't it a long time?" I asked him.
"Sure is, Scout," he said happily.

Jem's assumption is that a long deliberation is a good sign for the defendant.

Just when it feels like the waiting will go on forever, the clerk says:

"This court will come to order," in a voice that rang with authority, and the heads below us jerked up.

The suspense that extends over six pages is dispelled by action that occurs in less than two pages, in storytelling that is among the most powerful in American history.

What happened after that had a dreamlike quality: in a dream I saw the jury return, moving like underwater swimmers, and Judge Taylor's voice came from far away and was tiny. I saw something only a lawyer's child could be expected to see, could be expected to watch for, and it was like watching Atticus walk into the street, raise a rifle to his shoulder and pull the trigger, but watching all the time knowing that the gun was empty.

A jury never looks at a defendant it has convicted, and when this jury came in, not one of them looked at Tom Robinson. The foreman handed a piece of paper to Mr. Tate who handed it to the clerk who handed it to the judge...

I shut my eyes. Judge Taylor was polling the jury: "Guilty...guilty...guilty...guilty..." I peeked at Jem: his hands were white from gripping the balcony rail, and his shoulders jerked as if each "guilty" was a separate stab between them.

GENTLE SURPRISE

After consoling his client, Atticus grabs his coat and begins to leave the courtroom. As Scout stares down at the crowd from her seat:

Someone was punching me, but I was reluctant to take my eyes from the people below us, and from the image of Atticus's lonely walk down the aisle.

"Miss Jean Louise?"

I looked around. They were standing. All around us and in the balcony on the opposite wall, the Negroes were getting to their feet. Reverend Sykes's voice was as distant as Judge Taylor's:

"Miss Jean Louise, stand up. You father's passin'."

That ends the chapter and comes as a kind of surprise. All the waiting, all the clock watching, all the references to time, all the anticipation pointed us to the verdict. It turns out that only a shallow victory ensues: the length of deliberations. Jem should have listened to Reverend Sykes earlier in the chapter: "Now don't you be so confident, Mr. Jem, I ain't ever seen any jury decide in favor of a colored man over a white man." And they would not see it that day. What the children would see was an act of profound collective respect, a Greek chorus of colored citizens rising to their feet, not in the presence of an overseer but in tribute to one who stood for their common humanity. The author has played a beautiful trick on us. We thought we were looking for a verdict, but the real stab of the chapter comes later, hiding all the while in plain sight.

As we've seen with so many works thus far, there is great value in rereading a classic text over the course of years and decades. The racism of 2015 is different from the racism of 1960, when *Mockingbird* was published. The novel, while racially progressive and inspirational for its time, has been criticized for its characterization of white southern poverty and its depiction of the accuser of rape. Race, class, gender, region, and religion all play a role in the novel, and our perceptions of them have all evolved in the more than half century since publication. The word *nigger*—used dozens of times in the novel in the context of the 1930s—complicates a modern reading and teaching of the text. It is a healthy by-product of X-ray reading to think: "Times have changed" or "I have changed." That does not require us to ignore or discount the power of a work within the context of its own time. There is no way to explain away, for example, the anti-Semitism embedded in Shakespeare's *The Merchant of Venice*. That does not mean that we cannot recognize that Shakespeare has made Shylock more sympathetic than Christopher Marlowe's vicious Barabas in *The Jew of Malta*.

If you want the richest insight into southern racism in the twentieth century, read the testimony of African American authors. But the power of their words and the threads of their narratives in no way diminish the work of a young white southern woman, Harper Lee, whose story, drawn richly from her own childhood, continues to enlighten America and the world.

WRITING LESSONS

1. X-ray reading can detect and interpret texts that are embedded in other texts, such as the closing argument made by Atticus Finch to the all-white, all-male southern jury. This is a rousing, if seemingly futile, speech about democracy and justice, delivered with its own set of rhetorical flourishes, from the power of parallelism to emphatic word

order to the strategic use of the short sentence. All these tools are available to you as a writer and to the speakers who inhabit your work.

2. While there are no absolute requirements for telling good stories, time and again we see the benefits of certain strategies. One of them has been called a story engine—a question that only the story can answer. Some genres, such as the whodunit, come equipped with their own internal combustion engines. And remember that a story like *Mockingbird* raises and answers many important questions along the way.

3. The first picture I ever drew—my mother saved it—was the face of a clock. The ticktock structure of the transparent movement of time is among the most reliable narrative strategies. This structure has two beneficial effects. It can speed up time without transition as the narrative moves forward. Or, in the name of suspense, it can slow time down—often with the tool of shorter and shorter sentences, forcing the reader to wait and anticipate an outcome.

4. When suspense is resolved, there is often an opportunity for a surprise, an exploitation of the reader's expectations of what will come next. The author can create a twist or, better yet, an enhanced experience. We thought the high point of chapter 21 would be the verdict. In fact, the guilty verdict in the Jim Crow South was predictable. What followed was a more transcendent moment as the black citizens of the town stand to pay homage to the white lawyer.

21

X

X-raying M. F. K. Fisher

Cooking a Story

You have probably heard of most of the authors mentioned in this book, but you may not have heard of M. F. K. Fisher. She is well recognized as one of the great food writers of the last century, but many authors and readers, including Hemingway, thought she deserved greater fame than that. Fisher wrote about food, it is true, including cooking methods and recipes. But food was an open window rather than a closed door. Through it, she could see all aspects of civilization, culture, community, and family. In 1942 she wrote her most daring work, *How to Cook a Wolf*. That "wolf" was the Nazi menace. The war against the Third Reich required the rationing of goods and services. Fisher offered advice on how to eat well with less. She demonstrated how to support the war effort and how to take solace in the pleasure of eating, even with danger lurking.

Perhaps if Fisher could have cooked for Yeats, "The Second Coming" would have ended differently: "Slouching towards Bethlehem, Pennsylvania, where you can find a great Italian bakery."

Here's a passage from *How to Cook a Wolf:*

> Once when young Walter Scott, who later wrote so many exciting books, was exceptionally hungry and said happily, "*Oh,* what a fine soup! Is it not a *fine* soup, dear Papa?," his father immediately poured a pint of cold water into what was already a pretty thin broth, if the usual family menu was any sample. Mr. Scott did it, he said, to drown the devil.
>
> For too many nice ordinary little Americans the devil has been drowned, so that all their lives afterwards they eat what is set before them, without thought, without comment, and, worst of all, without interest. The result is that our cuisine is often expensively repetitive: we eat what and how and when our parents ate, without thought or natural hungers.

DOTING ON THE ANECDOTE

As I X-ray this passage, I see an opportunity to reflect upon the power of the anecdote. It's an odd and interesting word—*anecdote*—often misunderstood or mispronounced by adults and children alike as "antidote." To be sure, many an anecdote has proven to be an antidote to tedious or abstract writing. *The American Heritage Dictionary* defines it as "a short account of an interesting or humorous incident." Its etymology is Greek and means, literally, "not published." The sense is that an anecdote provides some special insight in a biography, some previously unknown bit that sheds light on a person's history or character.

In this century the anecdote has come under attack. In a sense, anecdotal evidence is the opposite—though, I would argue, not the enemy—of data analysis. The argument against the anecdote is that it may not represent with any accuracy a larger reality. Political debate, as we know too well, is filled with dueling anecdotes, each side offering a little story that tries to convince us of the truth of a point of view.

To return to Fisher's work, the anecdote that begins the passage gives the impression that Sir Walter Scott grew up in a harsh Scottish Presbyterian culture that saw common pleasures as occasions for sin. By adding water to the broth, the father diluted the simple pleasure of tasting it, "drowning the devil" along the way.

More interesting to writers is Fisher's next move, beginning with the sentence "For too many nice ordinary little Americans the devil has been drowned." Fisher repeats a key phrase from the end of one paragraph and places it at the beginning of the next. That connectivity has a name in rhetoric. It is called cohesion. An easy definition: cohesion is the effect we feel when the small parts of a work fit together. (When the large parts fit together, we call it something else: coherence.)

Fisher chooses to begin the passage with a Scottish anecdote, using it to caution us against American forms of puritanism and warning us that we do one another no good when we turn the pleasurable and nurturing act of eating into savorless routine and drudgery. Even more, we give aid and comfort to our enemies when we reduce our lives to spartan sacrifice. She writes:

> If, with the wolf at the door, there is not very much to eat, the child should know it, but not oppressively. Rather, he should be encouraged to savor every possible bite with one eye on its agreeable nourishment and the other on its fleeting but valuable esthetic meaning, so that twenty years later, maybe, he can think with comfortable delight of the little brown toasted piece of bread he ate with you once in 1942, just before that apartment was closed, and you went away to camp.

ROPES OF TROPES

Let's give a moment of attention to Fisher's repetition and variation of the phrase "with the wolf at the door," remembering that the title of her book is *How to Cook a Wolf*. I have two, perhaps three names for this move. Journalists might call it a conceptual scoop—an original idea that defines a pattern or trend in the news or popular culture. This is usually described with a handy word or catchphrase, such as "soccer mom" or "NASCAR dad" or "Gen Xer" or "tipping point" or "flat world." In straight language, Fisher's wolf is about how to live well and responsibly in a dangerous world.

But her language is not straight but crooked—a metaphor—and here is where we can borrow language from literary criticism to our advantage as writers. We can begin by calling the wolf a trope, which is, according to *The American Heritage Dictionary,* "a figure of speech using words in nonliteral ways, such as a metaphor." When that trope shows up again and again, as it does in Fisher's book, it becomes something else: a motif, that is, "a recurrent thematic element in an artistic or literary work" or "a dominant theme or central idea." This term is so useful that we can find it exemplified not only in literature but also in music and architecture.

Let me be transparent about how this works in my book. The title includes a trope—an image, a metaphor: *The Art of X-ray Reading.* It is meant to evoke everything from medical technology—looking through the body to see a person's skeleton—to Superman, with his superpower of X-ray vision, to those cheesy ads in comic books for "X-ray glasses." I have to remind myself to repeat the phrase "X-ray reading" or "X-ray vision" or "X-ray glasses" in every chapter so that the trope becomes a motif and the motif lends coherence to the whole, uniting the big parts.

Returning to Fisher, she moves constantly between the concept of food as a cultural artifact and the exquisite sensory experience of good eating, even with something as humble as a piece of toast and butter:

> It was a nice piece of toast, with butter on it. You sat in the sun under the pantry window, and the little boy gave you a bite, and for both of you the smell of nasturtiums warming in the April air would be mixed forever with the

savor between your teeth of melted butter and toasted bread, and the knowledge that although there might not be any more, you had shared that piece with full consciousness on both sides, instead of a shy awkward pretense of not being hungry.

Here Fisher offers us a vicarious adventure through a reliable writing strategy: using language that appeals to the senses. It is not necessary in such passages to appeal to all the senses, but any characterization beyond the standard visual description will create a special effect. Here we can see the butter and bread and pantry window, feel the warmth of the sun and the crunch between our teeth, smell the brilliant orange-yellow flowers, and, of course, taste the savory snack. See, feel, smell, taste. The sound is left to the imagination.

Fisher concludes her passage with a kind of reprise, a musical term that can be applied to writing, meaning "a repetition of a phrase or verse" or "a return to an original theme":

All men are hungry. They always have been. They must eat, and when they deny themselves the pleasures of carrying out that need, they are cutting off part of their possible fullness, their natural realization of life, whether they are poor or rich.

It is a sinful waste of human thought and energy and deep delight, to teach little children to pretend that they should not care or mention what they eat. How sad for them when they are men! Then they may have to fight, or love, or make other children, and they won't know how to do it fully, with satisfaction, completely, because when they were babies they wanted to say, "*Oh,* what a fine soup!" and instead only dared murmur, "More, please, Papa!"

What an astonishing affirmation of life, passion, creativity, and love, all seen through the lens of good eating. And, like so many of the writers we have X-rayed so far, Fisher returns at the end to the note she struck at the beginning, transforming what was a literary anecdote into a kind of declaration of independence. I'm not sure anyone who reads it can take an insignificant bite of food again. Enjoy.

RECIPE FOR WRITING

If you flip through the pages of *How to Cook a Wolf,* you will see spots where it looks like a cookbook. Economical and savory recipes abound. But no one has ever written a recipe the way Fisher can. She appropriates a form of instructional writing—a set of directions and ingredients—and kicks it up a notch in the literary sense. Here she is on a dish called riz à l'impératrice, or rice for the empress:

Wash, parboil, and then drain 1 pound of the finest rice. Slowly bake it with a vanilla bean, 1 quart of boiled rich milk, 2 cups fine white sugar, 1/4 pound fresh butter. Keep covered and do not stir. When still hot add gently the beaten yolks of 16 eggs (ah, that happy wolf…!) When cool add 1 cup minced candied fruits and 1 cup apricot jam, 1 pint thick English custard, and 1 pint whipped cream heavily flavored with Alsatian kirsch. Put a thick layer of red currant jelly in the bottom of a

Bavarian-cream mold, pour the above cream upon it, and let it chill thoroughly. To serve, turn out so that the jelly runs down over the firm sides. (This last is what sets off the cautious fireworks of reminiscence in my stomach-weary contemporaries who lived on such fatuous delicacies rather than my own grandmother's "plain boiled rice with cream and sugar.")

Even if you don't write recipes, look at all the things you can learn from this text:

- the power of the inventory (the list of ingredients)
- the importance of sequencing
- the power and beauty of names (Alsatian kirsch, Bavarian cream)
- the strong effect of imperative verbs (wash, parboil, drain, bake)
- the repetition of the trope ("that happy wolf")
- food as a spur to memory (remember what happened when Proust bit into a madeleine?)

WRITING LESSONS

1. Fisher builds her narrative around an organizing image, that of the hungry wolf. If there is a pattern of ideas or emotions in your work, it might be instructive to give the pattern a name. Advertising and marketing are filled with such images and tropes, leading to slogans such as "Where's the beef?" But these images can be the building blocks of great literature, either in fiction or nonfiction.

2. Make sure the big parts of your work fit together, giving it coherence. During revision make sure the small parts fit together as well, using such tools as repetition and conjunctions. The movement in sentences will often lead readers from something they already know at the beginning to some new knowledge at the end.

3. You can use anecdotes in at least two ways: (a) to prepare the reader for an idea and (b) to illustrate or exemplify an idea that's already been stated. If you present the anecdote first, the reader will wonder, why is he telling me that?, allowing you to gain a little altitude at the level of ideas. If the idea comes first, the reader will think, "I wish she would give me an example that I can see or feel."

4. Cooking and eating are sensory experiences, so it would be a wasted opportunity if a good writer did not use language that appeals to the senses of taste and smell. So much of what I write derives from visual experience that I often forget to include the other senses. Mark your writing for any elements that might appeal to the ear, skin, nose, and mouth.

5. Study nonliterary forms, such as the recipe, to learn lessons you can apply to literature and reportage—for example, listing, sequencing, and naming.

22

X

X-raying *Hiroshima*
Stopped Clock

On the lead-up to the year 2000, a series of retrospectives appeared in all media, a look back on the decade, century, millennium. A common method of expression was a list inviting us to recall and prioritize items within certain categories. What was the greatest American novel of the twentieth century? I'd vote for *The Great Gatsby.* What was the greatest song? "Over the Rainbow." Who was the greatest athlete? Babe Ruth or Muhammad Ali—I can't decide. What was the greatest nonfiction book? We have a lot to choose from, don't we? Perhaps *Silent Spring,* by Rachel Carson, or *The Other America,* by Michael Harrington. A number of the lists I noticed chose *Hiroshima,* by John Hersey.

The book was published in 1946, the year after the atomic bombing. It originally appeared in *The New Yorker,* which dedicated an entire issue to Hersey's story. Since then it has sold millions of copies, especially in a thin paperback edition that became and remains a staple for high school students. The world changed on August 6, 1945, and Hersey gave us all a view of what American forces had unleashed. It ended one war but ushered in the nuclear age.

A MOMENT IN TIME

Here is the first paragraph of *Hiroshima:*

> At exactly fifteen minutes past eight in the morning, on August 6, 1945, Japanese time, at the moment when the atomic bomb flashed above Hiroshima, Miss Toshiko Sasaki, a clerk in the personnel department of the East Asia Tin Works, had just sat down at her place in the plant office and was turning her head to speak to the girl at the next desk. At that same moment, Dr. Masakazu Fujii was settling down cross-legged to read the Osaka *Asahi* on the porch of his private hospital, overhanging one of the seven deltaic rivers which divide Hiroshima; Mrs. Hatsuyo Nakamura, a tailor's widow, stood by the window of her kitchen, watching a neighbor tearing down his house because it lay in the path of an air-raid-defense fire lane; Father Wilhelm Kleinsorge, a German priest of the Society of Jesus, reclined in his underwear on a cot on the top floor of his order's three-story mission house, reading a Jesuit magazine, *Stimmen der Zeit;* Dr. Terufumi Sasaki, a young member of the surgical staff of the city's large, modern Red Cross Hospital, walked along one of the hos-

pital corridors with a blood specimen for a Wassermann test in his hand; and the Reverend Mr. Kiyoshi Tanimoto, pastor of the Hiroshima Methodist Church, paused at the door of a rich man's house in Koi, the city's western suburb, and prepared to unload a handcart full of things he had evacuated from town in fear of the massive B-29 raid which everyone expected Hiroshima to suffer. A hundred thousand people were killed by the atomic bomb, and these six were among the survivors. They still wonder why they lived when so many others died. Each of them counts many small items of chance or volition—a step taken in time, a decision to go indoors, catching one streetcar instead of the next—that spared him. And now each knows that in the act of survival he lived a dozen lives and saw more death than he ever thought he would see. At the time, none of them knew anything.

Before we apply the discipline of X-ray reading, let's exercise a parallel discipline, literary accounting:

- The passage is one paragraph in length.
- It contains 347 words.
- It has seven sentences.
- The average sentence length is almost fifty words.
- The lengths of the seven sentences, in order, are: 65, 189, 17, 11, 31, 26, and 8 words.
- That longest sentence, at 189 words, is divided into five clauses and uses four semicolons and a period.
- The shortest sentence, the last one, begins with seven one-syllable words, the longest of which consists of four letters.

X-ray reading will help us use some of those numbers to calculate the literary and rhetorical effect upon the reader. Let's begin with the first sentence, which I'll divide into three parts: beginning, middle, and end.

BEGINNING

> At exactly fifteen minutes past eight in the morning, on August 6, 1945, Japanese time...

This feels like a most unconventional way to begin a story. In spite of the importance of time to the telling of all narratives, we rarely see this degree of temporal specificity in a first line. The word *exactly* is not a modifier but an intensifier. We then learn the minutes, the hour ante meridiem, the month, day, year, and time zone. That's seven discrete time metrics before a verb. The rhetorical effect of such specificity is that of a historical marker. Something world-changing is about to happen (a meteor struck the earth; a volcano exploded; a jet plane flew into the Pentagon). Chaucer's springtime at the beginning of *The Canterbury Tales* is generic and cyclical. In *Hiroshima* we are about to meet another group of pilgrims who share an experience that is triggered at a specific moment in time.

In a way, time is also about to stand still. Clocks and watches, damaged by the atomic blast, stopped at the moment of destruction. This symbol of the stopped watch in relation to Hiroshima is repeated as late as 2014 in the updated version of the movie *Godzilla*. The original was made in Japan in 1954 and is widely recognized as a science-fiction, monster-movie allegory of the consequences of nuclear destruction. In the updated version, Japanese actor Ken Watanabe carries around the talisman of a pocket watch owned by his grandfather, killed at Hiroshima. The time is frozen at eight fifteen.

MIDDLE

> ...at the moment when the atomic bomb flashed above Hiroshima...

I have argued many times that emphatic words in a sentence should go at the end. The middle is the location of least emphasis. You might think that an author writing about the dropping of the atom bomb would build up to that moment, not insert it almost as an afterthought (perhaps better described here as a beforethought). But contrary to expectations Hersey places the real heat of the sentence in the middle, almost casually, so we are taken by surprise.

This part of the sentence is best seen as an extension of the first, another time marker, a phrase followed by a clause, both of which act as adverbs answering the question "When?" The phrase "flashed above Hiroshima" deserves special attention. The common understanding about bombs dropped from planes is that they explode upon impact. They hit something and destroy it. One gets the sense of an awesome new technology with this language. A verb of light such as *flashed* reminds us not just of explosive destruction but also of radiation.

END

...Miss Toshiko Sasaki, a clerk in the personnel department of the East Asia Tin Works, had just sat down at her place in the plant office and was turning her head to speak to the girl at the next desk.

In bringing us finally to the main part of the sentence, the author puts into practice two reliable rhetorical strategies, one from ancient Greece, the other from the American newsroom. The name for the first is litotes, or understatement — the opposite of hyperbole. While an unwise writer might overwhelm us with the visceral imagery of destruction, Hersey chooses to introduce a most common scene of daily life: one office worker turning to another, allowing the drama to unfold. In the face of astonishing content, step back a bit. Don't call undue attention to the tricks of the writer.

A related strategy comes from an old bit of newsroom wisdom: "The bigger the smaller." Nowhere was this strategy more useful than in the aftermath of the terrorist attacks on New York City on September 11. Faced with almost apocalyptic physical destruction and the loss of nearly three thousand lives, writers such as Jim Dwyer of the *New York Times* looked for ways to tell a story that seemed from its inception "too big." Dwyer chose to highlight physical objects with stories hiding inside of them: a window washer's squeegee used to help a group break out of a stalled elevator in one of the Twin Towers; a family photo discovered in the rubble; a paper cup used by an escaping stranger to give water to another.

The author of *Hiroshima* offers readers something akin to writing teacher Robert McKee's "inciting incident." This is the moment that kicks off the energy of the story, the instant when normal life is transformed into story life. All the characters described in the first paragraph are experiencing a version of normal, everyday life — given the context of an ongoing world war — but whatever their expectations, they were changed forever at the exact moment the atomic bomb flashed over Hiroshima.

CAST OF CHARACTERS

Just as that first sentence has a beginning, a middle, and an end, so does the paragraph itself. Its beginning is the lead sentence that we X-rayed. The middle consists of a list of names, a catalog of characters — what is called in dramatic literature the dramatis personae, the people of the drama. There are six of them, including Miss Sasaki, all with Japanese names except the German Jesuit, Father Kleinsorge. They are introduced to us with stylish efficiency, not just with titles or job descriptions but also with actions appropriate to their state (it would be interesting to hold up these descriptions against the language that introduces Chaucer's pilgrims). It's the ordinariness of their actions that will contrast with the extraordinary circumstances of their survival. A clerk chats with another girl; a doctor settles on his porch; a widow gazes from her window; a priest reads a religious magazine; a surgeon walks down a hospital corridor; a pastor unloads a cart of clothing.

The ending of the first paragraph constitutes a component of nonfiction writing that is now commonly referred to as the nut. The nut—sometimes a sentence, paragraph, section—answers the question: "Why am I reading this?" Or, more particularly: "Why am I reading about these people and this place?" The news is already known: an atomic bomb flashed over Hiroshima. But what comes next? What consequences? What subsequent narratives? These six characters—in spite of their countless personal differences—share something in common: they survived the worst bombing in human history.

The author lays it out, sentence by sentence:

"A hundred thousand people were killed by the atomic bomb, and these six were among the survivors." Here is a nicely balanced sentence, two independent clauses joined to establish a contrast between death and survival, between a large number and a small one.

"They still wonder why they lived when so many others died." A fascinating sentence, a consequence of actions yet to be described. A collective experience that has a common name: survivor's guilt.

"Each of them counts many small items of chance or volition—a step taken in time, a decision to go indoors, catching one streetcar instead of the next—that spared him." Another expression of shared experience. To give readers a sense of the whole, the writer uses three examples. There are six characters, but there could just as well be seven or twenty-nine (the number of pilgrims in *The Canterbury*

Tales). Those three examples tell you everything you need to know.

"And now each knows that in the act of survival he lived a dozen lives and saw more death than he ever thought he would see." The word *now* stands for the time after the bombing, after the crises of survival, after the writing is done. The characters collectively look back on what they have endured. The scenes of endurance will constitute the story.

"At the time, none of them knew anything." As so often happens, the shortest sentence comes last and has the ring of gospel truth. At the end of a long and detailed paragraph, the short sentence almost functions as punctuation, as a signifier of closure and understanding. With the phrase "At the time," the author returns us to the opening sentence, the moment when clocks would break and time would stand still.

WRITING LESSONS

1. Stories are about time in motion. But there are moments when time seems to stop, at least in narrative terms: when the atom bomb drops, when Kennedy is shot, when the *Challenger* explodes. As a writer, you can mark that moment when time stands still. Freeze a movie into a still frame.

2. A good way to begin a long story is to list the key characters or issues or events at the top. Give readers enough to generate interest. You are saying, in effect: "If you want to know more about the German Jesuit, read on." Make a promise at the beginning. Fulfill it by the end.

3. Shakespeare's plays begin with a list of characters— the dramatis personae, the people of the drama. It's a good

strategy for many reports and stories. Name the people (or dogs, penguins, or whales) who will populate the work. Now, here is the key question: In what order will they appear? Who will walk onstage first? Hersey begins with two clerks at the moment of the explosion. Then his six characters are presented in outline, not unlike the way Chaucer presents the Canterbury pilgrims.

4. Given the nature of the news and the death toll, the author's narrative feels somehow underwritten, but in a good way. There are no elaborate metaphors. The author keeps the focus on the cast of characters and not on his own feelings or emotions. In general, this is a good rhetorical strategy. The more powerful or consequential the content, the more the author should "get out of the way." This does not mean that craft must be set aside. Instead, it means craft must be used to create a feeling of understatement.

23

X

X-raying Rachel Carson and Laura Hillenbrand

Sea Inside Us

One vicious stereotype about women writers is that they excel at writing about romance and relationships. My antidote to that propaganda is to point to the excellence of women writers themselves and to two women in particular — writing around fifty years apart — whose work shines in its coverage of subjects usually associated with men: science and sports.

MAGICAL CLARITY

In 1950 Rachel Carson wrote the book *The Sea Around Us*, a work so powerful that it won a National Book Award and was turned into a documentary film that won an Oscar. It is a thin text of 166 pages. Because of its brevity and scientific content, it was assigned to countless high school students in the 1950s and '60s, not unlike *Hiroshima,* by John Hersey.

Carson was a remarkable stylist whose work deserves revisiting and whose exquisite prose lends itself to a full examination via X-ray reading. Check out this passage on the enduring legacy of the sea carried within the bodies of land animals:

> When they went ashore the animals that took up a land life carried with them a part of the sea in their bodies, a heritage which they passed on to their children and which even today links each land animal with its origin in the ancient sea. Fish, amphibian, and reptile, warm-blooded bird and mammal—each of us carries in our veins a salty stream in which the elements sodium, potassium, and calcium are combined in almost the same proportions as in sea water. This is our inheritance from the day, untold millions of years ago, when a remote ancestor, having progressed from the one-celled to the many-celled stage, first developed a circulatory system in which the fluid was merely the water of the sea.

I've reread that passage about half a dozen times just to swim around in it. That is often the first step for me as a reader. I find myself immersed in a passage that does something special to me or for me. At times it is the satisfaction of an aesthetic impulse, the appreciation of a beautiful-sounding collection of words. At other times it is an effect of powerful content, helping me see myself or the universe in a surprising new way. I am suddenly remembering an ancient rhetorical precept that the purpose of great literature is *docere et delectare*—to instruct and delight. And of course in the best cases (as with most of the passages we are studying in this book), a classic work of literature will deliver both instruction and delight.

With my X-ray specs on, I see that I am responding at first to the power of an intellectual insight offered in this passage. Carson's title may be *The Sea Around Us,* but if this paragraph is any indication, it might be more accurately called *The Sea Inside Us.* After I first read this passage, I could never think of my body and the fluids inside of it the same way again.

But I am also beginning to see the strategies Carson calls upon to make this happen. Let me sort them out:

• Technical language instructs us but never dominates the common discourse. The tone is established in that first sentence of forty-seven common words, thirty-six of them of one syllable.

• The easy pace of ordinary language in the first sentence builds our muscles for the second sentence, which contains two simple scientific lists: one of categories of animals, the other of minerals.

• With that knowledge under our belts, we are armed for the third sentence, which contains the most technical bit of science, requiring us to understand the progression of animals from one-celled to many-celled and the development of their circulatory systems from seawater.

• Not one of these three sentences is short, but together they are so organized, logical in their progression, and coherent that they make powerful sense.

LANGUAGE AND LOGIC

Let's look at another passage from Carson that is so clear it's almost translucent, once again a product of her language and logic:

> Nowhere in all the sea does life exist in such bewildering abundance as in the surface waters. From the deck of a vessel you may look down, hour after hour, on the shimmering discs of jellyfish, their gently pulsating bells dotting the surface as far as you can see. Or one day you may notice early in the morning that you are passing through a sea that has taken on a brick-red color from billions upon billions of microscopic creatures, each of which contains an orange pigment granule. At noon you are still moving through red seas, and when darkness falls the waters shine with an eerie glow from the phosphorescent fires of yet more billions and trillions of these same creatures.

If it is the author's purpose to make us see, it would be hard to imagine a passage that accomplishes this with greater clarity than Carson's. In the previous text, her goal was to make us see in the intellectual sense—that is, to understand. "I once was blind, but now I see" has both an optical and cognitive implication.

Carson's passage has some "efferent" content in it, to be sure—knowledge readers can carry away. We learn that the sea is full of things we can see on its surface, and we learn some of their names. We learn about shapes in the sea and colors and lights. But the language is different in this passage, more mysterious and poetic, more to be read aloud in the company of others. Here we get "shimmering discs" and "pulsating bells." We get "brick-red color," a surprising one for the sea, along with "orange pigment granule." We get the contrast of the falling darkness and the shining of the sea. We get "eerie glow" and, best of all, the alliterative "phosphorescent fires," four syllables modifying one. The repetition of the word *billions,* followed by *trillions,* creates a kind of planetarium effect.

ALTITUDE AND DEPTH

Such epiphanic work deserves a great ending, and Carson delivers:

In its broader meaning, that other concept of the ancients remains. For the sea lies all about us. The commerce of all lands must cross it. The very winds that move over the lands have been cradled on its broad expanse and seek ever to return to it. The continents themselves dissolve and pass to the sea, in grain after grain of eroded land. So the rains that rose from it return again in rivers. In its mysterious past it encompasses all the dim origins of life and receives in the end, after, it may be, many transmutations, the dead husks of that same life. For all at last return to the sea—to Oceanus, the ocean river, like the ever-flowing stream of time, the beginning and the end.

There is a true majesty in this prose, created by the accumulation of phrases such as "commerce of all lands," "mysterious past," "ever-flowing stream of time," and especially the final prayerlike evocation of the alpha and the omega, "the beginning and the end." Hiding in the middle is my favorite sentence in this paragraph: "So the rains that rose from it return again in rivers." There are eleven words in that sentence, and all the key words begin with the letter *r*, yet it took me several readings to notice the alliteration. In linguistics the letter *r* is called a liquid consonant. Carson's ear would have told her that "rains...rose...return...rivers"—the repetition of those *r*'s—would make the passage flow. Given the content of the paragraph, what better vehicle of expression than repetition of a liquid letter?

SLOW-MOTION RIDER

What Rachel Carson did for marine biology, Laura Hillenbrand accomplished for horse racing. As I describe at length in my book *The Glamour of Grammar*, whenever we concentrate on the *rules* of grammar and punctuation, we run the risk of veiling the creativity and flexibility available to authors who think of them as *tools* of meaning and effect.

Let's take as an example a splendid passage from Hillenbrand's bestselling book *Seabiscuit*, an instant classic, a stirring narrative history of one of America's legendary racehorses. In this scene, Hillenbrand describes the mystical glory of

Seabiscuit's last great stretch run in the 1940 Santa Anita Handicap:

> In the midst of all the whirling noise of that supreme moment, Pollard [the jockey] felt peaceful. Seabiscuit reached and pushed and Pollard folded and unfolded over his shoulders and they breathed together. A thought pressed into Pollard's mind: *We are alone.*
>
> Twelve straining Thoroughbreds; Howard and Smith in the grandstand; Agnes in the surging crowd; Woolf behind Pollard, on Heelfly; Marcella up on the water wagon with her eyes squeezed shut; the leaping, shouting reporters in the press box; Pollard's family crowded around the radio in a neighbor's house in Edmonton; tens of thousands of roaring spectators and millions of radio listeners painting this race in their imaginations: All this fell away. The world narrowed to a man and his horse, running.

Consider all the tools of language used — and not used — to create this startling, cinematic slow-motion effect. Not used, for example, are commas to break up what might look like a run-on sentence: "Seabiscuit reached and pushed and Pollard folded and unfolded over his shoulders and they breathed together." You will find three independent clauses in that sentence without the hint of a comma. You could argue that the brevity of these clauses makes punctuation unnecessary, even intrusive. I would suggest a more literary effect — that the sentence describes a continuous flowing action of horse and jockey: first horse, then jockey, then both together. The action, if you will, is running on. And so is the sentence.

Then something startling happens, marked by the sentence in italics: *"We are alone."* The author considers this thought so important, so dramatic, that she emphasizes it in three ways: she expresses it in the shortest possible sentence; she places it at the end of a paragraph, next to a bar of white space; and she takes advantage of the convention of setting a character's thoughts in italic type.

What follows is an exercise in literary and cinematic time management, a slow-motion effect that expands the moment in the service of suspense. Each of the eight phrases leading to the final main clause ("all this fell away") happens in an instant as the camera pans from the track to the grandstand to the stables to the press box to a house in Canada to an audience of millions around the world. Unlike the earlier sentence, this is not one continuous motion but simultaneous action, the literary equivalent of a cinematic montage. Here commas would not be strong enough to enclose the distinct actions. Periods would insult their spontaneity. The solution: that oft-maligned expression of Aristotle's golden mean, the semicolon. Seven of them, to be exact.

The final, startling insight comes in the form of one triumphant sentence: "The world narrowed to a man and his horse, running." The movement is from a big noun (*world*) to two particular nouns (*man* and *horse*) that resolve themselves in a single word, a present participle (*running*), which, standing at the end of the sentence, connotes perpetual motion...immortality.

As I was working on this chapter, a friend pointed me to a profile of Hillenbrand written by Wil S. Hylton for the *New York Times Magazine*. It contains an anecdote that offers one of the best examples of X-ray reading and its benefits I have ever seen. It is spoken by Daniel James Brown, author of the bestselling book about the 1936 U.S. Olympic rowing team, *The Boys in the Boat.* He describes what he learned from Hillenbrand and *Seabiscuit:*

> When I first started *The Boys in the Boat*—I mean, the day after I decided to write the book—I had an old paperback copy of *Seabiscuit,* and we were going on a vacation.... So I threw it in my suitcase, and I spent the whole vacation dissecting it. I put notes on every page in the book, just studying all the writerly decisions she had made: why she started this scene this way and that scene that way, and the language choices in how she developed the setting.... One of the things I wrote down in the margins of the book was that I needed to do this or I needed to do that.... I went into the whole research project with a list of guidelines, which were drawn from this close study of *Seabiscuit.*

What powerful testimony. Brown may use the phrase "close study" to describe his learning process as a writer, but we would call it X-ray reading.

WRITING LESSONS

1. Ease your reader into anything complex. If the tough parts come too soon, the reader can become discouraged. If, on the other hand, you build the interest of the reader with, say, anecdotes or poetic language, the reader will have faith in you and follow you into the thicket.

2. Test paragraphs of explanation to make sure they are built upon some logic: chronology, geography, size, complexity. Use the paragraph as a building block of narrative, explanation, or argument. Paragraphs work best when they develop a single, startling, memorable idea, such as the notion that each of us carries the sea inside of us.

3. Ask yourself, how quickly do I want this passage to move? Think in cinematic terms when you need to figure out if you want to create full motion or if you would prefer slow motion. In general, the faster you want a sentence to go, the less punctuation you will use. Every mark of punctuation slows a passage down to some degree. Think of your period as a British "full stop" and your comma, perhaps, as a "half stop." The semicolon is somewhere in between.

4. Use Daniel James Brown's anecdote about Laura Hillenbrand as a map. Before you begin a big writing project, find a model that works for you. X-ray it, marking your thoughts in the margins. Underline the reporting and writing strategies that might benefit your work.

24

X

X-raying Toni Morrison
Repetitious Variation

Some writers are great storytellers; others are great lyricists. Nobel laureate Toni Morrison is both, of course, but when reading *The Bluest Eye* I found myself wanting to stop the narrative so that I could rest and savor the beauty and power of her prose. It's like that rare occasion when you stop the car trip for a minute so you can watch the sun set behind the mountain.

There are countless passages that deserve our close attention, but there is one Morrison move that stands out. For lack of a better word, I will call it repetition, which we have discussed more than once in this book. I don't mean repetition in its common sense—using a word or phrase over and over again until it gets tedious or meaningless. Morrison's texts might look like that at first glance, but upon

X-ray inspection it turns out that each signature word changes with repetition, like an echo in a valley.

Let's revisit the distinction between repetition and redundancy. The first, remember, tends to be intentional, purposeful, reinforcing. The latter is needlessly repetitive, a waste of words and space. No one told the Beatles that "She loves you, yeah, yeah, yeah" didn't need all those "yeahs." But when we use the cliché "various and sundry," it's not hard to recognize that both words mean about the same thing. "Please go sit on that sofa or couch," said the redundant shrink.

Before we look at passages from Morrison, a plot summary would be helpful. The book, set in 1940–41, tells the story of a young black girl, Pecola Breedlove, who is obsessed with white images of beauty. In an act of racial and personal self-loathing, she dreams of having the bluest eyes. She suffers the cruelties of poverty, rape, and a pregnancy that ends in stillbirth, sustained only by a fantasy of blue eyes — fulfilled when she becomes possessed by mental illness in the end. Written in 1962, Morrison's work anticipates decades of attention to racial beauty, diversity, feminism, body image, and sexual abuse.

RIGHT WORDS IN THE RIGHT ORDER

Let's begin by X-raying a single narrative sentence that is central to the thematic action of the story:

Each night, without fail, she prayed for blue eyes.

As I did earlier with a line from *Macbeth* ("The Queen, my lord, is dead"), I'll begin by creating alternative versions of the original. Morrison could have written:

- Without fail, each night she prayed for blue eyes.
- She prayed for blue eyes each night without fail.
- She prayed for blue eyes without fail each night.
- For blue eyes she prayed each night without fail.

When I study the work of a Nobel Prize winner, I am inclined to give her the benefit of the doubt. So let's X-ray the parts of Morrison's version:

- "Each night"—This may seem at first a weak, adverbial way to begin a sentence until we realize the significance of "night"—the time of darkness, dreams, nightmares, fantasies, memories, and projections of our future.
- "without fail"—Isn't this redundant with "each night"? If I tell you I do something each night, doesn't that imply I do it every time? Here is where a bit of redundancy intensifies the meaning, adds depth and dimension. "Without fail" speaks to obsession, the seed for mental illness, the idea that if she did not perform this action it would be deemed a failure.
- "she prayed for"—The verb could have been *hoped* or *dreamed*. Instead it is stronger. She "prayed" for it. That prayer reminds us of an innocent child who says her prayers at bedtime ("Now I lay me down to sleep..."), but that connotation of innocence is destroyed time and again by the

damage others inflict upon Pecola, which transforms into the harm she does to herself.

- "blue eyes"—I often find great writers taking advantage of this move: putting the most interesting, important, or emphatic words near the end of a sentence. I would love to know how many times the word *eyes* or the phrase "blue eyes" appears in the novel. (I just opened the novel at five random pages, and either the word *blue* or the word *eyes* appeared at least once on each page.) Since *The Bluest Eye* is the title of the book, and since the desire for blue eyes stands as the engine of the narrative, it makes perfect sense that the language would be repeated, just as the phrase "my girl" is repeated over and over by the Temptations in Smokey Robinson's famous song.

TITLE TO FOCUS

For years I have been preaching that every piece of writing needs a focus, a central theme or thesis, a point that all the evidence in that text will somehow support. For Morrison it's right there in the title, *The Bluest Eye*. That imagined transformation of Pecola's natural brown eye color is the "objective correlative" that T. S. Eliot identifies as a central concern of the poet. The blue eye becomes the object that correlates to the dominant theme or issue or concern the author is trying to express. In a 1993 afterword to the novel, Morrison writes, "Implicit in her [Pecola's] desire was racial self-loathing. And twenty years later I was still wondering about how one learns that. Who told her? Who made her feel that it was better to be a freak than what she was? Who had looked at her and found her so wanting, so small a weight on the beauty scale? The novel pecks away at the gaze that condemned her."

Let's X-ray a passage narrated by a character named Claudia, who describes the moral, cultural, and economic conditions of her time and place via the repetition of a single signature word:

> Outdoors, we knew, was the real terror of life. The threat of being outdoors surfaced frequently in those days. Every possibility of excess was curtailed with it. If somebody ate too much, he could end up outdoors. If somebody used too much coal, he could end up outdoors. People could gamble themselves outdoors, drink themselves outdoors. Sometimes mothers put their sons outdoors, and when that happened, regardless of what the son had done, all sympathy was with him. He was outdoors, and his own flesh had done it. To be put outdoors by a landlord was one thing—unfortunate, but an aspect of life over which you had no control, since you could not control your income. But to be slack enough to put oneself outdoors, or heartless enough to put one's own kin outdoors—that was criminal.

The word *outdoors* appears eleven times in this paragraph of 138 words. It appears eleven times in ten sentences. It appears in every sentence except the third. It appears in different locations: at the beginning of a sentence, at the end, and in the middle. The word *outdoors* can be used as a noun or adjective, but more often it appears as an adverb (as it does in each use above).

THE SAME, BUT DIFFERENT

Repetition craves variation, an effect that often comes with parallel constructions. I work from a simple definition of parallelism: the use of similar words or phrases to discuss similar things or ideas. Notice, for example, how these two sentences parallel each other:

> If somebody ate too much, he could end up outdoors.
> If somebody used too much coal, he could end up outdoors.

These are the same, but different. Morrison can manage this in a single sentence as well: "People could gamble themselves outdoors, drink themselves outdoors." "Gamble themselves" parallels "drink themselves," and both point to the word *outdoors*.

You would think that this level of repetition might exhaust the topic, but not so. In the very next paragraph, Morrison builds on her dominant theme, but uses it to gain some altitude—that is, to move from the world, where things are happening, to a higher place, where meaning is discovered:

> There is a difference between being put *out* and being put out*doors*. If you are put out, you go somewhere else; if you are outdoors, there is no place to go. The distinction was subtle but final. Outdoors was the end of something, an irrevocable, physical fact, defining and complementing our metaphysical condition. Being a minority in both

caste and class, we moved about anyway on the hem of life, struggling to consolidate our weaknesses and hang on, or to creep singly up into the major folds of the garment. Our peripheral existence, however, was something we had learned to deal with — probably because it was abstract. But the concreteness of being outdoors was another matter — like the difference between the concept of death and being, in fact, dead. Dead doesn't change, and outdoors is here to stay.

Five more uses of the word *outdoors,* but how different they are from those in the first paragraph. There the emphasis was on "outdoors" as a physical place. In the following paragraph the word has climbed up the ladder of abstraction, assuming the status of a condition of being, a way of life. The stakes get higher and higher until "outdoors" is not just a form of alienation or ostracism but also a virtual equivalent of death. "Dead doesn't change, and outdoors is here to stay."

WRITING LESSONS

1. Embrace the distinction between repetition and redundancy. Use the first to establish a pattern in the work, whether of language or imagery. Redundancy is not always a bad thing. (Redundant systems on an airplane keep it in the air, even if one system breaks down.) For the reader, you may want to create a variety of entry points to a single destination.

2. When you repeat a word, phrase, or other element of language or narrative, make sure it is worth repeating. Make sure that each repetition advances the story in some way.

Ineffective repetition slows down a narrative. Effective repetition helps it gain traction. Each reappearance of a character or repetition of a phrase can add meaning, suspense, mystery, or energy to a story.

3. Use strategies such as variation and parallelism to link key elements and to make each repetition memorable.

4. Good stories have a focus, a theme, a central idea, a governing metaphor—such as "the bluest eye." The eyes are the windows to the soul; the focus is the window to the soul of the story. If you find a powerful governing idea, it is almost impossible to make too much of it. The key, according to writer and editor William Blundell, is to repeat the focus but express it in different ways: through a character detail, a scene, a bit of dialogue.

25

X

X-raying Charles Dickens and Donna Tartt

Echo of Text

All writers should understand a literary concept called inter-textuality. This is a happy term — one that defines itself. It emerged as particularly important in the field of cultural studies and postmodern literary criticism where scholars and linguists argued that a written text is less a description of an objective world than it is a complicated mosaic of previous texts. This is not a euphemism or rationalization for acts of plagiarism. It is, instead, a recognition that long before an adult author has written a first novel, she has read hundreds of others. From those readings she has learned not just the grammar of written language but also the grammar of stories. There are all kinds of ways, good and bad, that she will use this knowledge in her writing, especially through clichés, allusions, parodies, responses, tropes, analogies, parallel constructions, and archetypes.

When done poorly, intertextuality that references other works feels derivative, lacking originality. When done well, it adds an extra layer of meaning, pointing from specific elements of plot to larger literary and cultural patterns and values.

ART ECHO

I'd like to simplify all these forms of influence into a single word: *echoes.* X-ray reading, tuned to the max, turns out to be a great method for recognizing both intended and unintended forms of influence that echo through an author's work.

Let's begin with the work of a contemporary author, Donna Tartt: the book is *The Goldfinch,* which won a Pulitzer Prize for fiction in 2014. This is an ambitious work of 771 pages, dense at times in its textual imagery and expansive in its cast of characters and its sense of time and place. I will summarize plot elements, including pieces of the ending, showing you what you need to see without spoiling the linear experience of the narrative.

Here's a paragraph from the jacket flap:

It begins with a boy. Theo Decker, a thirteen-year-old New Yorker, miraculously survives an accident that kills his mother. Abandoned by his father, Theo is taken in by the family of a wealthy friend. Bewildered by his strange new home on Park Avenue, disturbed by schoolmates who don't know how to talk to him, and tormented above all by his longing for his mother, he clings to the one thing that reminds him of her: a small, mysteriously captivating painting that ultimately draws Theo into the criminal underworld.

Before I began to read the novel, I knew that the author, Donna Tartt, was a deep and avid reader of classic literature, especially novels of the nineteenth century. "She's obsessed with Dickens," was the judgment of one editor, and you don't have to travel far into her novels without spotting the footprints of the author of such works as *Bleak House.* Among his literary gifts, Dickens is known for the brilliance of his characterization, creating worlds in which a rich variety of fascinating characters collide or collaborate to reveal troubling or hopeful messages about the social order. Tartt has some of that same gift, and it is clearly visible in *The Goldfinch.* Theo Decker (who has a bit of Holden Caulfield in him) is a young Dickensian hero, an orphan, struggling to find his place in the world, tossed on the seas of life between influences that seek to hurt him or help him.

It just so happened that while I was reading *The Goldfinch* I was also reading, on my iPad, a book called *The Man Who Invented Christmas,* by Les Standiford, a study of the life and work of Charles Dickens, with a special emphasis on the astonishing influence of *A Christmas Carol,* arguably the most popular and retold narrative in the history of literature in English. (If that analysis seems overstated, try to think of a competitor.)

It was Kurt Vonnegut, remember, who advised writers to choose a likable character and then spend hundreds of pages doing terrible things to him to see what he's made of. That describes the predicament of Theo Decker throughout *The Goldfinch*. In a journey that takes him from childhood into adulthood and carries him from New York City to a suburb of Las Vegas to the streets of Amsterdam, Theo faces everything from acts of terrorism to forms of drug addiction to exposure to dangerous criminal elements at home and abroad. But the inciting incident comes early — an explosion in an art museum that kills his precious mother. All other catastrophes become an afterthought.

So it's no surprise that any form of redemption will come to Theo through the memory of his mother. It happens in a dream late in the novel, on page 724, in a gorgeous piece of writing:

> Because all of a sudden, there she was. I was standing in front of a mirror and looking at the room reflected behind me.... And when I looked away for a second and then looked back, I saw her reflection behind me, in the mirror. I was speechless. Somehow I know I wasn't allowed to turn around — it was against the rules, whatever the rules of the place were — but we could see each other, our eyes could meet in the mirror, and she was just as glad to see me as I was to see her. She was herself. An embodied presence. There was psychic reality to her, there was depth and information. She was between me and whatever place she had stepped from, what landscape

beyond. And it was all about the moment when our eyes touched in the glass, surprise and amusement, her beautiful blue eyes with the dark rings around the irises, pale blue eyes with a lot of light in them: hello! Fondness, intelligence, sadness, humor. There was motion and stillness, stillness and modulation, and all the charge and magic of a great painting. Ten seconds, eternity.

What is going on here? I wondered as I read this passage. Or, more specifically: What does this remind me of? If I had the literary equivalent of a Geiger counter, it would have been clicking.

The main clue had been repeated over hundreds of pages of the novel. Theo's weird and wonderful Russian pal, Boris, had taken to calling Theo by the name Potter because of his resemblance to the young hero of the Harry Potter stories, by J. K. Rowling. If you know those books, you know that Harry was orphaned in infancy, his parents taken by the evil wizard Voldemort. What Harry Potter and Theo share is a terrible longing for loving parents and for home. Harry, of course, lives in a magic world, and he discovers in the first book a magical invention called the Mirror of Erised (*Desire* spelled backwards). The first time he gazes into that mirror he sees a reflection of his dead parents. They are so real he can almost touch them. At least for a moment it fills the empty space in his heart. In the words of his mentor, the great wizard Albus Dumbledore, the mirror "shows us nothing more or less than the deepest, most desperate desire of our hearts." For Theo, this desire is to be at one with his mother, and because he lives in a world without magic, she must come to him in a dream. As soon as I read the passage, I wrote in the margins, "Harry Potter's mirror."

But wait: there's more. On the very next page, Tartt writes,

> When I opened my eyes, it was morning. All the lamps in the room were still blazing and I was under the covers with no memory of how I'd gotten under them. Everything was still bathed and saturated with her presence—higher, wider, deeper than life, a shift in optics that had produced a rainbow edge, and I remember thinking that this must be how people felt after visions of saints—not that my mother was a saint, only that her appearance had been as distinct and startling as a flame leaping up in a dark room....
>
> Then, suddenly, bursting into the last wisps of bioluminescence still trailing from the dream, the bells of the nearby church broke out in such violent clangor that I bolted upright in a panic, fumbling for my glasses [another Harry Potter trope]. I had forgotten what day it was: Christmas.

I marked the passage and wrote in the margin: "Oh, shit. It's *A Christmas Carol*." Maybe it was because I had been reading the biography of Dickens. Or perhaps it was Tartt's reputation for attachment to Dickensiana. I ran to my copy of *A Christmas Carol* to revisit the familiar and inspiring passage. Ebenezer Scrooge awakens from a night of visitation by the spirits of Christmas past, present, and future. Full of hope, he sticks his head out the window and asks a wee lad below what day it is. Christmas. "It's Christmas Day!" said Scrooge to himself. "I haven't missed it." As if to confirm the reality of being awakened and transformed, Dickens describes an awe-inspiring sound: "He was checked in his transports by the churches ringing out the lustiest peals he had ever heard. Clash, clash, hammer; ding, dong, bell.... Oh, glorious, glorious!" And then: "Running to the window, he opened it, and put out his head. No fog, no mist; clear, bright, jovial, stirring, cold; cold, piping for the blood to dance to; Golden sunlight; Heavenly sky; sweet fresh air; merry bells. Oh, glorious. Glorious!"

You can decide from your own X-ray reading whether there are echoes of this scene in a parallel passage from Tartt:

> Unsteadily, I got up and went to the window. Bells, bells. The streets were white and deserted. Frost glittered on tiled rooftops; outside, on the Herengracht, snow danced and flew. A flock of black birds was cawing and swooping over the canal, the sky was hectic with them, great sideways sweeps and undulations as a single, intelligent body, eddying to and fro, and their movement seemed to pass into me on almost a cellular level, white sky and whirling snow and the fierce gusting wind of poets.

Revisit the pattern: descent into the destructive element, visitation by spirits, waking up from dreams on a Christmas morning, the tintinnabulation of bells, the throwing open of the window, the invigoration of the senses, the change of heart. Here is the key to recognizing a vigorous and creative form of intertextuality: *There are many more differences than similarities between the passages.* One invokes or evokes the other. One echoes the other — with more than a bit of magic thrown in for good measure.

One of the more interesting bits of scholarship on the subject comes from an essay by James E. Porter entitled "Intertextuality and the Discourse Community." He argues that intertextuality refers to

> the "repeatability" of certain textual fragments, to citation in its broadest sense...not only explicit allusions, references, and quotations within a discourse, but also unannounced sources and influences, clichés, phrases in the air, and traditions. That is to say, every discourse is composed of "traces," pieces of other texts that help constitute its meaning.... "Once upon a time" is a trace rich in rhetorical presupposition, signaling even to the youngest reader the opening of a fictional narrative. Texts not only refer to but in fact *contain* other texts.

One more example will suffice. As I was drafting this chapter, I found myself using a word I had never used before: *tintinnabulation.* It's a word that supposedly echoes the sound of the ringing of bells. That would have been good enough. But I also remember where I first heard it — in a classroom discussion of a well-known poem by Edgar Allan Poe, "The Bells." Technically, my own "tintinnabulation of bells" is redundant because that is what the longer word means, but for those who did not know it or recognize an allusion to the dark poet, I let a bit of repetition do its job.

The true art of intertextuality resides, finally, in figuring out what to include and what to leave out — whether to ring the bell loud and long or to muffle its sound to something soft and subtle.

WRITING LESSONS

1. As you think about your story, what other stories are you reminded of?

2. Are there useful elements you can draw — without plagiarism — from these influential texts?

3. How much of such influence will you want to share with the reader, and with what degree of transparency?

4. What elements of influence can you take advantage of? Tone, language, setting, theme, details?

5. Do you want your echoes to be loud or soft? If your readers do not recognize your echo, is your literal meaning and the context sufficient to make the passage clear and comprehensible?

GREAT SENTENCES FROM FAMOUS AUTHORS

An Exercise in X-ray Reading

In 2014 the editors of *The American Scholar* chose "ten best sentences" from literature, and readers suggested many more. This lovely feature caught me in the middle of writing a first draft of *The Art of X-ray Reading*. I am publishing here a collection of my own favorite sentences — some from *The American Scholar* and some from the books on my shelf. Each of these "mentor" sentences will appear on a right-hand page with plenty of white space around it. Use that space to mark up the page. Circle, underline, draw arrows, make connections. Write in the margins, noting what you see with your X-ray vision. After you've had a go at it, turn the page. On the back you will find my close reading of the text.

If you really want to hear about it, the first thing you'll probably want to know is where I was born, and what my lousy childhood was like, and how my parents were occupied and all before they had me, and all that David Copperfield kind of crap, but I don't feel like going into it, if you want to know the truth.

—J. D. Salinger, *The Catcher in the Rye*

J. D. Salinger sacrifices his own language and mature insights (sort of) to turn his narration over to a prep-school student, Holden Caulfield, who came to represent the alienation of the post–World War II generation. This is a carefully constructed text, but it doesn't sound that way. It sounds like someone talking. How do you do that? You use the second person ("you"), contractions ("you'll"; "don't"), slang ("lousy"), intensifiers ("really"), verbal punctuation ("and all"), and mild profanity ("crap"). The cumulative effect is informal and conversational.

Salinger had a great ear for the spoken word and captures the idioms of his time in phrases such as "how my parents were occupied" and "if you want to know the truth." A double-edged razor hides in both phrases. The first one could mean "what my parents did for a living," but "occupied" carries with it some negative connotations, as in the word *preoccupied*.

The second phrase, about truth, is used mostly as filler in conversation, yet the key word, *truth,* comes at the end, raising the question of whether Holden is a reliable narrator of his own life story. My favorite phrase here is "and all that David Copperfield kind of crap." Note the alliteration, the repetition of hard *c* sounds. Perhaps Holden sees himself as a Dickensian character, like David Copperfield, who experiences an endless series of traumatic events in his young life. Or perhaps the reclusive author is sending a secret signal: just as *David Copperfield* is considered Dickens's most autobiographical novel, *Catcher* contains, we now know, many parallels to the young life of J. D. Salinger.

In such condition there is no place for industry, because the fruit thereof is uncertain: and consequently no culture of the earth; no navigation nor use of the commodities that may be imported by sea; no commodious building; no instruments of moving and removing such things as require much force; no knowledge of the face of the earth; no account of time; no arts; no letters; no society; and, which is worst of all, continual fear and danger of violent death; and the life of man solitary, poor, nasty, brutish, and short.

—Thomas Hobbes, in *Leviathan,* on what happens to human beings during a state of war

This is the most famous sentence written by Hobbes in his most famous book. He writes a generation after Shakespeare, and there is that rhythm and weight we hear so often in passages from the King James Bible. The key word in the passage is its shortest: *no.* For the record, it appears ten times in a sentence of only ninety-two words. War, whatever the stated intentions of those who wage it, is nihilistic, a negation of the human.

That word, *no,* connects the elements of the first of the sentence's two great inventories, the one that defines the building blocks of culture and civilization: industry, agriculture, navigation, construction, cartography, art, literature, and society. (When I gaze in the twenty-first century at parts of the world imperiled by war and terrorism, I mourn not just what is destroyed but also what might have been constructed or imagined in a time of peace.)

But more powerful in a time of war than our incapacities is the propinquity of violence and death, leading to Hobbes's second inventory, this one adjectival—descriptions of the life of humans beings in such circumstances: solitary, poor, nasty, brutish, and short. That final word lands like a heavy stone dropped upon a table.

Before the aurora borealis appears, the sensitive needles of compasses all over the world are restless for hours, agitating on their pins in airplanes and ships, trembling in desk drawers, in attics, in boxes on shelves.

—Annie Dillard, *Pilgrim at Tinker Creek*

I admire the way Dillard turns a piece of natural science into a narrative of anticipation during which no human being makes an entrance. The aurora borealis, better known as the northern lights, is a spectacular display of colors caused by solar winds interacting with Earth's magnetic fields. (That is a simplified description of a complex process.) Before that vision occurs across the northern sky, its presence can be detected—in this case not by sophisticated electronic equipment but by a simple compass, the invention we use so often as a metaphor for moral direction. Through her quick inventory, Dillard moves us from very big things to very small—from planes and ships to objects that can fit in desk drawers and in boxes on shelves, where human beings cannot even see them. They are put away. But while people are inattentive and insensitive, the needles of compasses are highly responsive—restless, agitated, and trembling.

I returned, and saw under the sun, that the race is not to the swift, nor the battle to the strong, neither yet bread to the wise, nor yet riches to men of understanding, nor yet favour to men of skill; but time and chance happeneth to them all.

—Ecclesiastes 9:11, King James Version

The writing in this famous passage is so good that George Orwell wrote a parody of it designed to ridicule the bloated writing of his day: "Objective consideration of contemporary phenomena compels the conclusion that success or failure in competitive activities exhibits no tendency to be commensurate with innate capacity, but that a considerable element of the unpredictable must invariably be taken into account." Orwell's parody is based on an X-ray reading of what makes the original so good. Of the forty-nine words in the biblical original, forty-one are of one syllable, including sturdy Anglo-Saxon words such as *sun, race, swift, strong, bread, wise, skill,* and *time.* In an early sequence, twelve consecutive words have one beat. That might create a tedious staccato rhythm were it not for the inclusion of parallel patterns: race to the swift, battle to the strong, bread to the wise, and so forth. The sentence begins with subject and verbs: I returned...and saw. But the real bolt strikes at the end, when the meaning of the sentence moves from the power of human beings to the things they cannot control: time and chance. What the heck were they drinking back in Elizabethan and Jacobean England? I would love a sip of that writer's brew.

But some day we may have a genuinely democratic govern-ment, a government which will want to tell people what is hap-pening, and what must be done next, and what sacrifices are necessary, and why.

— George Orwell, "Propaganda and Demotic Speech"

When it comes to political language, Orwell is better known as a critic than an exemplar. That's too bad, because the author of "Politics and the English Language," which emphasizes the kind of writing and speech we should avoid, often writes texts that serve as counterexamples, such as the one above. I'm tempted to divide the sentence into two parts, right between the two uses of the word *government*. The first is the object of a one-two-three main clause: subject, verb, object: "But some day we may have a genuinely democratic government." Look at all that conditional language at the front end ("some day"; "may have"). But what does Orwell mean by "democratic"? It is a question that requires a definition of the word. We would recognize such a government by its actions, as defined and described in the second part of the sentence. There, Orwell gives us a recipe for democratic speech, the parts stitched together with the most basic words: *what, what,* and *why*. That is a reliable strategy: through repetition and parallel structures, establish a pattern, but then change it at the end, in this case from what to why.

Past the flannel plains and blacktop graphs and skylines of canted rust, and past the tobacco-brown river overhung with weeping trees and coins of sunlight through them on the water downriver, to the place beyond the windbreak, where untilled fields simmer shrilly in the A.M. *heat: shattercane, lamb's-quarter, cutgrass, sawbrier, nutgrass, jimsonweed, wild mint, dandelion, foxtail, muscadine, spinecabbage, goldenrod, creeping charlie, butter-print, nightshade, ragweed, wild oat, vetch, butcher grass, invaginate volunteer beans, all heads gently nodding in a morning breeze like a mother's soft hand on your cheek.*

—David Foster Wallace, *The Pale King*

This sentence is so hard to read that its greatness is debated. I have found it listed among the best and worst sentences ever written, and it does convey a look-at-me quality that some critics find self-indulgent. But make believe, for a second, that you love it. Take a ride across a symbolic American landscape, populated by (count them) twenty species of weed and wild plant—each with a wonderful name. There is a bizarre flyover quality to it—cinema by way of Salvador Dalí. The first half places us on a blimp, where we view a decaying cityscape. Then the blimp turns into a crop duster as we swoop down across a field of weeds. But back to Dalí: there is a docent nearby to name each one for us. The effect is vertigo, dislocation, a view through the looking glass. Can a sentence be great but not good?

There was some one thing that was too great for God to show us when He walked upon our earth; and I have sometimes fancied that it was His mirth.

—G. K. Chesterton, *Orthodoxy*

This is the final sentence of Chesterton's most important book on Christian faith. Chesterton was a writer of great versatility, able to craft with equal vigor a detective story and a theological essay. Both, perhaps, involve mystery. This sentence walks the line between the most traditional and the most unconventional expressions of religious faith. The capital letters in *He* and *His* represent the traditional theology of Jesus Christ as the Son of God. As the embodiment of the divine, Jesus earns the uppercase. But that same theology emphasizes that Christ is fully God and fully human, which leads the author to a highly unusual description of Jesus: one who had "mirth." We don't use that word much to describe "merriment accompanied by laughter," as one dictionary defines it. Nor do we use *fancied,* meaning "imagined." What stands out is the surprising rhyme between *earth* and *mirth.* Both are one-syllable words that vibrate at the end of independent clauses. Yet the words look so different, as if they shouldn't rhyme. A rhyme in prose rarely works, I think, because it calls so much attention to that echo. Here it does not intrude. It feels like two hands clapping.

No single gesture would do more to demonstrate continuity and stability—to show that the government of the United States would continue to function without interruption despite the assassination of the man who sat at its head—and to legitimize the transition: to prove that the transfer of power had been orderly, proper, in accordance with the Constitution; to remove, in the eyes of the world, any taint of usurpation; to dampen, so far as possible, suspicion of complicity by him in the deed; to show that the family of the man he was succeeding bore him no ill will and supported him, than the attendance at this swearing-in ceremony of the late President's widow.

—Robert A. Caro, *The Passage of Power*

The great presidential biographer Robert Caro has proved countless times that he understands the power of a short sentence. His description of the instant in Dallas that changed LBJ's—and America's—life forever is told in just six words: "There was a sharp, cracking sound."

Contrast that to the 115 words in the example above. Notice that it contains the two qualities that characterize good long sentences. It takes us on a journey of sorts, not across a landscape, as in the David Foster Wallace example, but across a plan of action. And it contains an inventory, not of physical objects but of a set of purposes. It adds a final element, though: a body of evidence. The case is made early and late in the sentence that after JFK's assassination, the best way to show the peaceful transfer of power in America was by the presence of Jacqueline Kennedy at LBJ's swearing-in ceremony. Every word within that frame is designed to convince.

And I add my own love to the history of people who have loved beautiful things, and looked out for them, and pulled them from the fire, and sought them when they were lost, and tried to preserve them and save them while passing them along literally from hand to hand, singing out brilliantly from the wreck of time to the next generation of lovers, and the next.

—Donna Tartt, *The Goldfinch*

Two famous English actors, both of whom played Macbeth, were discussing how to deliver the great soliloquy, the one that begins "Tomorrow and tomorrow and tomorrow." The veteran actor advised the younger one, "Remember that the most important word is *and*." That surprising insight may apply as well to Donna Tartt's sentence. It begins with "And," which some word puritans consider taboo. There are six *and*s in all, as if the first one announced that this would be an exercise in language accumulation. This sentence comes near the end of a long novel and strikes a thematic note, even as the narrator summarizes the meaning of his own experiences. What I especially appreciate is the kind of blending of realistic and metaphorical elements. The narrator did love beautiful things, did pull one from the fire, did look out for it, did seek it when it was lost, and so on. Action phrases, such as "pulled them from the fire" and "hand to hand," coexist with phrases like "the wreck of time." The sense is of a single character as part of a long historical line, one that goes back centuries and looks ahead to more of the same.

If the history of the earth's tides should one day be written by some observer of the universe, it would no doubt be said that they reached their greatest grandeur and power in the younger days of Earth, and that they slowly grew feebler and less imposing until one day they ceased to be.

—Rachel Carson, *The Sea Around Us*

Few authors have written as magnificently about nature as Rachel Carson, and this sentence is a good example. Its strength is not in form but content. It reveals to me something I did not know—that at one time in the history of Earth, the tides were much more powerful than they are today. They have grown weaker (as a result of the moon drifting farther from Earth, as it turns out, decreasing its gravitational influence), and they will grow weaker and weaker over millions of years until one day they will cease to be. That shocking phrase at the end is the result of a distinctive writing strategy. I'll call it "the impossible narrator." Look at the premise at the beginning: a history of tides will be written "by some observer of the universe." Who is such an observer? God? An alien creature? An earthling who has migrated to another galaxy? It does not matter. What matters is that Carson found an elegant vehicle for communicating an amazing reality of the cosmos.

This private estate was far enough away from the explosion so that its bamboos, pines, laurel, and maples were still alive, and the green place invited refugees — partly because they believed that if the Americans came back, they would bomb only buildings; partly because the foliage seemed a center of coolness and life, and the estate's exquisitely precise rock gardens, with their quiet pools and arching bridges, were very Japanese, normal, secure; and also partly (according to some who were there) because of an irresistible, atavistic urge to hide under leaves.

— John Hersey, *Hiroshima*

Great writers fear not the long sentence, and here is proof. If a short sentence speaks a gospel truth, then a long one takes us on a kind of journey. This is best undertaken when subject and verb come at the beginning, as in this example, with the subordinate elements branching to the right. There is room here for an inventory of Japanese cultural preferences, but the real target is that final phrase, an "atavistic urge to hide under leaves," even in the shadow of the most destructive technology ever created, the atomic bomb.

It was a fine cry—loud and long—but it had no bottom and it had no top, just circles and circles of sorrow.

—Toni Morrison, *Sula*

I did not know this sentence, chosen by the editors of *The American Scholar,* but I love it. It expresses a kind of synesthesia, a mixing of the senses, in which a sound can also be experienced as a shape. Add to this effect the alliteration of *loud* and *long,* and the concentric movement of sound in "circles and circles of sorrow," and we have something truly memorable.

For what do we live, but to make sport for our neighbors, and laugh at them in our turn?

—Jane Austen, *Pride and Prejudice*

Who could not admire a sentence with such a clear demarcation of beginning, middle, and end? Thank you, commas. Only a single word—*neighbor*—has more than one syllable. Austen gives us nineteen words that add up to sixty-seven letters, an astonishing efficiency of fewer than four letters per word. But this math is invisible to the meaning. She begins by asking what at first seems like a metaphysical question: "For what do we live?" The social commentary that follows brings us crashing to earth in a phrase and carries us home with a delicious sense of revenge, a kind of sophisticated punch line.

Anger was washed away in the river along with any obligation.

— Ernest Hemingway, *A Farewell to Arms*

Donald Murray used to preach the two-three-one rule of emphasis. Place the least emphatic words in the middle. The second most important go at the beginning. The most important nail the meaning at the end. Hemingway offers a version of that here. A metaphor of flowing water is framed by two abstractions: anger and obligation. The fact that the metaphor is drawn from the action of the narrative makes it more effective.

There are many pleasant fictions of the law in constant operation, but there is not one so pleasant or practically humorous as that which supposes every man to be of equal value in its impartial eye, and the benefits of all laws to be equally attainable by all men, without the smallest reference to the furniture of their pockets.

—Charles Dickens, *Nicholas Nickleby*

Old sentences can feel ornate. Mostly gone from our diction is the euphuistic style—long, intricately balanced sentences that show off the brilliance of the writer but ask too much of the reader. But in Dickens the sentence as argument feels just right. In short, it says that poor men cannot hope for justice. It does so by an act of civic demythologizing, hitting the target again with the memorable final phrase, "the furniture of their pockets."

In many ways he was like America itself, big and strong, full of good intentions, a roll of fat jiggling at his belly, slow of foot but always plodding along, always there when you needed him, a believer in the virtues of simplicity and directness and hard labor.

—Tim O'Brien, *The Things They Carried*

Again we see how a long sentence can flow from work done near the beginning: "he was like America itself." Such a simile always evokes an instant question from the reader: "How was he like America itself?" The answer combines description and allegory. He was a living microcosm of American strength and weakness. In an unusual turn, the most interesting element rests in the middle, with "a roll of fat jiggling at his belly."

There is nothing more atrociously cruel than an adored child.

—Vladimir Nabokov, *Lolita*

This sentence has the ring of familiarity to it, perhaps because it's Nabokov's riff on *King Lear:* "How sharper than a serpent's tooth it is / To have a thankless child!" *Lolita* may have more great sentences than any novel I know, but I'm not sure this is one of them. I worry about any sentence that uses an adverb for a crutch. *Cruel* is not enough for Humbert Humbert. He must magnify the cruelty with a word— *atrociously*—that denotes wickedness. It's not the child's fault she is adored, yet this makes her an atrocity. Now that I have thought it through, it sounds exactly like Humbert's self-delusions after all: blaming the victim. Perfect.

Like the waters of the river, like the motorists on the highway, and like the yellow trains streaking down the Santa Fe tracks, drama, in the shape of exceptional happenings, had never stopped there.

—Truman Capote, *In Cold Blood*

We used to call this a periodic sentence—that is, one in which the main action occurs at the period. Any word that comes right before the period gets special attention. The effect is magnified by the boxcar alignment of those opening similes, along with the shift from things we can see to something abstract—drama. Which never stopped there, of course. Until it did.

TWELVE STEPS TO GET STARTED
AS AN X-RAY READER

1. Begin with your routine habits, reading for information or the experience of story.

2. Look for passages that make you stop, not because they are bad but because they are so good that you want to enjoy and appreciate them.

3. Read these "showstopper" passages again, this time more slowly.

4. Look for the part of the passage you like best: it could be a paragraph, a sentence, a metaphor, even a word.

5. Read that part again, this time aloud. If there is another person in the room, read it aloud to that person.

6. If the passage comes from a book or magazine, mark it with a pencil, then write some words or phrases in the margins that describe what interests you.

7. Ask yourself, out loud if it helps, "How did the writer do this?"

8. Put on your metaphorical X-ray glasses and see if you can answer that question.

9. If you are having trouble coming up with an answer, share the passage with friends, colleagues, teachers.

10. Duplicate the passage—you may even want to copy it by hand to get a feel for it—and save it in a journal or file.

11. Put the passage away and begin your own writing. You don't need to imitate the model text. It's better if the influence is indirect.

12. If you discover a technique or strategy not mentioned in this book, add it to your copy of *The Art of X-ray Reading*. (And send it to me! rclark@poynter.org.)

ACKNOWLEDGMENTS

X

In less than a decade, I have produced five books on writing, reading, language, and learning for one of the world's best publishers: Little, Brown. I like to brag that I have the same publisher as Emily Dickinson, Louisa May Alcott, Evelyn Waugh, John Fowles, J. D. Salinger, Ansel Adams, David Foster Wallace, and—oh, did I mention Emily Dickinson? I'm having fun, of course, but when I see that list of authors and artists, it feels strange to be a member of their club, the one branded Little, Brown (please don't forget that comma).

Personal thanks go to Michael Pietsch and Reagan Arthur for their great leadership at the Hachette Book Group and LB and for being champions of authors, publishers, and book lovers everywhere. What a blessing to have worked with my editor, Tracy Behar, on five books now. With me, at least, she has a magic touch. Great copyediting lives at LB, thanks to Betsy Uhrig and Barbara Clark. I am a lucky author to have had Keith Hayes design the covers for all five of my books. I implore readers everywhere: please, please judge my books by their fabulous covers.

Special thanks go to my agent, Jane Dystel—she deserves her own paragraph—a figure of wisdom and stability in my professional life.

All my work has been supported, for almost forty years, by the leaders of the Poynter Institute, the influential school for journalism and democracy in St. Petersburg, Florida. My colleagues, especially Tom French, help me learn something new about the writing craft every day. My writing students—of all ages—remind me of my mission and purpose. Please visit the Poynter website and its News University for resources for writers: poynter.org and newsu.org. Feel free to contact me at rclark@poynter.org.

While finishing a draft of this book, I received a phone call from one of my favorite writers on writing, William Zinsser, just before he passed away. Bill was the author of *On Writing Well*, a work that has sold more than a million copies. At the age of ninety-two, Bill was going strong. Though blind, he visited with aspiring writers in his Manhattan apartment and was working with a young tutor to learn how to write poetry. We reminisced about our occasional stints working together, going back to Poynter's early days. I thanked him for everything he had done for writers, and he left me with this thought: "Let's keep this mission going." That mission is to recognize good writing wherever we see it, to encourage young writers to embrace the craft, and to remind everyone of the enduring power of the written word—all done in the spirit of democracy and in the public interest. Yes, let's keep that mission going.

To the members of my family, I say thanks once again: Shirley, Vincent, Theodore, Alison, Deeds, Emily, Dan, Lauren, Chaz, Donovan, and—remembering the requirements of emphatic word order, putting the most important or interesting word at the end—Karen.

SUGGESTED READING

X

One purpose of this book is to nudge you gently to the reading of some of the best literature ever written. Below you will find a list of books studied in *The Art of X-ray Reading*. In almost every case, I direct you to an inexpensive and widely available edition, not necessarily the one I quote from in the text. Read. Enjoy. X-ray. Write.

Simon Armitage, translator. *Sir Gawain and the Green Knight.* New York: W. W. Norton, 2007.

Jane Austen. *Pride and Prejudice.* New York: Penguin, 2003.

Truman Capote. *In Cold Blood.* New York: Vintage, 2012.

Robert A. Caro. *The Passage of Power.* New York: Vintage, 2012.

Rachel Carson. *The Sea Around Us.* New York: Oxford University Press, 1991.

Geoffrey Chaucer. *The Canterbury Tales.* Translated by Nevill Coghill. New York: Penguin, 2003.

G. K. Chesterton. *Orthodoxy.* New York: Ortho Publishing, 2014.

Charles Dickens. *Bleak House.* New York: Penguin, 2003.

———. *A Christmas Carol.* New York: Simon and Schuster, 2007.

Joan Didion. *Slouching Towards Bethlehem.* New York: Farrar, Straus and Giroux, 1990.

Annie Dillard. *Pilgrim at Tinker Creek.* New York: Harper-Perennial, 1998.

Jennifer Egan. *A Visit from the Goon Squad.* New York: Anchor Books, 2011.

M. F. K. Fisher. *How to Cook a Wolf.* New York: Farrar, Straus and Giroux, 1988.

F. Scott Fitzgerald. *The Great Gatsby.* New York: Scribner, 2004.

Gustave Flaubert. *Madame Bovary.* Translated by Lowell Bair. New York: Bantam, 1989. (Contains essay by Eric Auerbach.)

Gabriel García Márquez. *One Hundred Years of Solitude.* Translated by Gregory Rabassa. New York: Harper-Perennial, 2006.

Ernest Hemingway. *A Farewell to Arms.* New York: Scribner, 2012.

John Hersey. *Hiroshima.* New York: Vintage, 1989.

Laura Hillenbrand. *Seabiscuit.* New York: Ballantine Books, 2001.

Thomas Hobbes. *Leviathan.* New York: Penguin, 1982.

Homer. *The Iliad of Homer.* Translated by Richmond Lattimore. Chicago: University of Chicago Press, 1961.

———. *The Odyssey.* Translated by Robert Fitzgerald. New York: Farrar, Straus and Giroux, 1998.

Zora Neale Hurston. *Their Eyes Were Watching God.* New York: HarperPerennial, 2013.

Shirley Jackson. *The Lottery and Other Stories.* New York: Farrar, Straus and Giroux, 2005.

James Joyce. *Dubliners.* Mineola, N.Y.: Dover, 1991.

———. *A Portrait of the Artist as a Young Man.* Mineola, N.Y.: Dover, 1994.

———. *Ulysses.* New York: Penguin, 2008.

Harper Lee. *To Kill a Mockingbird.* New York: Grand Central, 1988.

Herman Melville. *Moby-Dick.* New York: Penguin, 2009.

Toni Morrison. *The Bluest Eye.* New York: Penguin, 1994.

———. *Sula.* New York: Vintage, 2004.

Vladimir Nabokov. *Lolita.* New York: Vintage, 1989.

Tim O'Brien. *The Things They Carried.* New York: Penguin, 1990.

Flannery O'Connor. *The Complete Stories.* New York: Farrar, Straus and Giroux, 1971.

George Orwell. *All Art Is Propaganda.* New York: Mariner, 2008.

Camille Paglia. *Break, Blow, Burn.* New York: Pantheon, 2005.

Sylvia Plath. *The Bell Jar.* New York: HarperPerennial, 2005.

Philip Roth. *Goodbye, Columbus.* New York: Vintage, 1994.

J. D. Salinger. *The Catcher in the Rye.* New York: Little, Brown, 2001.

William Shakespeare. *King Lear.* New York: Simon and Schuster, 2005.

———. *Macbeth.* New York: Simon and Schuster, 2003.

———. *Othello.* New York: Simon and Schuster, 2004.

———. *Romeo and Juliet.* New York: Simon and Schuster, 2004.

John Steinbeck. *The Grapes of Wrath*. New York: Penguin, 2006.

Donna Tartt. *The Goldfinch*. New York: Little, Brown, 2013.

Helen Vendler. *The Art of Shakespeare's Sonnets*. Cambridge: Harvard University Press, 1997.

Virgil. *The Aeneid*. Translated by Robert Fagles. New York: Viking, 2006.

David Foster Wallace. *The Pale King*. New York: Little, Brown, 2012.

Nathanael West. *Miss Lonelyhearts & The Day of the Locust*. New York: New Directions, 2009.

William Butler Yeats. *The Collected Poems*. New York: Scribner, 1996.

INDEX

Index

Bennett, Tony, 44
Bergman, Ingrid, 146
Bible, King James, 274, 277–78
biblical references, 33, 34, 76, 139,
    191, 193, 194–95, 201
Bleak House (Dickens), 156–58,
    159, 264
Bluest Eye, The (Morrison), 253–59
Blundell, William, 260
Boccaccio, Giovanni, 94
Boys in the Boat, The (Brown), 250
"Brainless" (song; Eminem), 31
Break, Blow, Burn (Paglia), 71
Breaking Bad (TV series), 50
Brown, Dan, 36
Brown, Daniel James, 250, 252
Bruccoli, Matthew J., 20
Buffy the Vampire Slayer (TV
    series), 7, 94
"Business" (song; Eminem), 31

Cain, James, 7
Canterbury Tales, The (Chaucer),
    35, 80, 93–94, 121, 149–59
    compared to *Hiroshima*, 236,
        240–41, 242
Capote, Truman, 305–6
Capra, Frank, 94
Carey, James, 57–58
Caro, Robert A., 285–86
Carraway, Nick *(The Great Gatsby),*
    13–14, 20, 22–23, 34
Carson, Rachel, 64, 233, 243–48,
    289–90
Catcher in the Rye, The (Salinger), 7,
    53–54, 271–72
catharsis, 133
Cather, Willa, 64
"Caught in the Web" (newspaper
    series; Frye), 122
characters
    gatherings of, 93–95, 99, 166
    motivation of, 107–8, 110

names and, 39, 89
plots and, 126–27
presentation of, 239–42
revealed by objects, 89
stock, 87–88, 89
Chaucer, Geoffrey, 35, 42, 46, 93–94
    See also *Canterbury Tales, The*
Chekhov's gun (narrative device), 81
Chesterton, G. K., 283–84
children's literature, 189
Christmas Carol, A (Dickens), 263,
    266–67
cinematography, 142–43, 145–48,
    168, 249, 250, 252, 282
Clark, Lauren, 184, 186
Clark, Roy Peter
    Glamour of Grammar, The, 8, 248
    "Three Little Words," 122
coherence, 226, 228, 232, 246
cohesion, 226
Collins, Suzanne, 98
colors, 25
comedy, 100, 128, 134
connotations, 5, 14, 25, 75, 133, 210–11
Conrad, Joseph, 141, 148
consonants
    fricative, 5–6
    interdental, 30
    liquid, 5–6, 31, 32, 211, 248
    plosive, 5–6
    sibilant, 5, 30, 73
context
    historical, 221–22
    meaning and, 196, 204
contranyms, 53
conversational effect, 272
"Conversion of the Jews, The"
    (Roth), 146–47
Cooper, Anderson, 31
Cooper, Gary, 218
Cooper, James Fenimore, 189
copying passages, 13, 187, 308
Corrigan, Maureen, 11–12

ABOUT THE AUTHOR

X

By some accounts, Roy Peter Clark is America's writing coach, a teacher devoted to creating a nation of writers. A PhD in medieval literature, he is widely considered the most influential writing teacher in the rough-and-tumble world of newspaper journalism. With a deep background in traditional media, Clark has illuminated the discussion of writing on the Internet. More than two million of his podcasts on the craft have been downloaded. He has gained fame by teaching writing to children and has nurtured Pulitzer Prize–winning authors such as Thomas French and Diana Sugg. He is a teacher who writes and a writer who teaches.

For more than three decades, Clark has taught writing at the Poynter Institute, a school for journalists in St. Petersburg, Florida, considered among the most prominent such teaching institutions in the world. He graduated from Providence College in Rhode Island with a degree in English and earned a PhD from Stony Brook University.

In 1977 he was hired by the *St. Petersburg Times* (now the *Tampa Bay Times*) to become one of America's first writing coaches and worked with the American Society of Newspaper Editors to improve newspaper writing nationwide. He was inducted into the Features Hall of Fame, an honor he shares with the likes of Ann Landers. He has served as the William Starr Writer-in-Residence at Vassar College, an honor he shares with authors such as Billy Collins, Tim O'Brien, and Salman Rushdie. He has received an honorary doctorate from Goucher College.

Clark has written or edited eighteen books about writing and journalism, including his most recent, *How to Write Short*.